Public Enemies: Al Capone, John Dillinger, Bonnie & Clyde, and Baby Face Nelson

By Charles River Editors

About Charles River Editors

Charles River Editors was founded by Harvard and MIT alumni to provide superior editing and original writing services, with the expertise to create digital content for publishers across a vast range of subject matter. In addition to providing original digital content for third party publishers, Charles River Editors republishes civilization's greatest literary works, bringing them to a new generation via ebooks.

Sign up here to receive updates about free books as we publish them, and visit Our Kindle Author Page to browse today's free promotions and our most recently published Kindle titles.

Introduction

Al Capone (1899-1947)

On February 14, 1929, members of Bugs Moran's North Side gang arrived at a warehouse on North Clark Street in Chicago, only to be approached by several police officers. The officers then marched them outside up against a wall, pulled out submachine guns and shotguns, and gunned them all down on the spot. A famous legend is that one of the shot men, Frank Gusenberg, dying from 14 gunshot wounds, told police that nobody shot him. Though Gusenberg's statement is probably apocryphal, nobody opened their mouths.

Nobody was ever convicted for the "Saint Valentine's Day Massacre," the most famous gangland hit in American history, but it's an open secret that it was the work of America's most famous gangster, Al Capone. Indeed, "Scarface" has captured the nation's popular imagination since Prohibition, managing to be the most notorious gangster in America while living a very visible and high profile life in Chicago.

Born a Brooklyn tough, Capone engaged in a life of crime even as a teenager and had come to Chicago as a young man to smuggle liquor during Prohibition. Allying himself with Johnny Torrio, Capone began to accumulate power almost as quickly as he accumulated a reputation for being merciless, and after an attempted hit severely injured Torrio, the gang's operations were turned over to Capone.

Despite his organized crime spree during the '20s, Capone was a popular figure in Chicago, viewed by many as a Robin Hood because he took pains to make charitable donations to the city. At the same time, he bribed government officials and cops, ensuring they looked the other way despite his violent ways of doing business. Throughout the decade, Capone was often out in public, despite several attempts on his life, and the gang war between Al Capone and Bugs Moran was well known and even celebrated to an extent.

In the end, it wasn't the bodies or the violence that landed Capone in the slammer; it was taxes. After being convicted, Capone managed to continue running his business rackets from behind bars, forcing authorities to move America's most notorious gangster to America's most notorious prison on Alcatraz Island. Capone and Alcatraz only added to each other's lore.

Capone died in 1947, but his life and legacy continue to be the stuff of legends. Even to this day, Chicago's gangster past is viewed as part of the city's lore, and tours of the most famous spots in Chicago's gang history are available across the city. *Public Enemies* looks at the life and crime of Scarface, and the manner in which he has become and remain a staple of American pop culture. Along with pictures of Capone and important people, places, and events in his life, you will learn about America's most infamous gangster like you never have before.

John Dillinger (1903-1934)

"I will be the meanest bastard you ever saw when I get out of here." – John Dillinger

America has always preferred heroes who weren't clean cut, an informal ode to the rugged individualism and pioneering spirit that defined the nation in previous centuries. The early 19th century saw the glorification of frontier folk heroes like Davy Crockett and Daniel Boone. After the Civil War, the outlaws of the West were more popular than the marshals, with Jesse James and Billy the Kid finding their way into dime novels. And at the height of the Great Depression in the 1930s, there were the "public enemies", common criminals and cold blooded murderers elevated to the level of folk heroes by a public frustrated with their own inability to make a living honestly.

Two months after Franklin D. Roosevelt's inauguration in 1933, a petty thief who had spent almost a decade behind bars for attempted theft and aggravated assault was released from jail. By the end of the year, that man, John Dillinger, would be America's most famous outlaw: Public Enemy Number One. From the time of his first documented heist in early July 1933, until his dramatic death in late July of the following year, he would capture the nation's attention and imagination as had no other outlaw since Jesse James.

His exploits were real, and in many cases impressive, but Dillinger's importance and legacy have always been partly symbolic. The country was in a panic over a supposed crime wave that some historians believe was more perception than reality, but a new breed of criminal targeting the nation's already vulnerable banks was a potent illustration and metaphor of the way society's institutions and morals seemed to be coming undone. And in the mind of the public, the outlaws of the 30s were very different from the gangsters of the 20s; they hailed from the farm country of America's nostalgic past, not the corrupt cities of its unsettled present and scarier future. Much was made of Dillinger's roots in the farming town of Mooresville, Indiana, even though he came of age in Indianapolis, and was very much a city boy at heart.

Ultimately, the story of Dillinger and the era's other famous criminals—Bonnie and Clyde, Baby Face Nelson, Pretty Boy Floyd—would largely be seen as a story of America's fall from grace. Just before Dillinger was released from prison in 1933, a feature article ran entitled "The Farmer Turned Gangster." America saw in Dillinger what it wanted to see, and even in Dillinger's lifetime it was nearly impossible to separate myth from reality.

Even still, Dillinger would never have become the mythical figure he became if J. Edgar Hoover and the FBI hadn't actively marketed him as "Public Enemy Number One," and if he hadn't died in a way that was almost scripted for Hollywood. Dillinger's figure looms so large in American history and popular culture that it's easy to forget that his starring role in the daily news lasted for less than a year.

Public Enemies looks at the life and crime of the famous outlaw, but it also humanizes him and analyzes his lasting legacy. Along with pictures of Dillinger and important people, places, and events in his life, you will learn about the infamous public enemy like you never have before.

Baby Face Nelson (1908-1934)

"He had a baby face. He was good looking, hardly more than a boy, had dark hair and was wearing a gray topcoat and a brown felt hat, turned down brim." –The wife of Chicago Mayor Big Bill Thompson describing the man who attacked her and stole her jewelry in October 1930.

The man who became Public Enemy Number One after the deaths of John Dillinger and Pretty Boy Floyd was Lester Joseph Gillis, whose alias "George Nelson" eventually gave way to the nickname "Baby Face Nelson". Despite the almost playfully innocent nickname, and the fact that he was not as notorious as two of his partners in crime, Dillinger and Floyd, Baby Face Nelson was the worst of them all.

In an era where the outlaws were glorified as Robin Hood types, Baby Face was a merciless outlier who pulled triggers almost as fast as he lost his temper. By the time fate caught up with Baby Face Nelson in November 1934 at the "Battle of Barrington", a shootout that left his body riddled with nearly 20 bullet holes, he was believed to have been responsible for the deaths of more FBI agents than anybody else in American history. It was a distinction he would have appreciated; during one bank robbery, Baby Face Nelson gleefully screamed "I got one!" after shooting police officer Hale Keith several times.

Due to his association with Dillinger and his own crime spree, Baby Face Nelson became a fixture of pop culture and was the main character in a few Hollywood films two decades after his death. Though he is not remembered as colorfully as Dillinger or Bonnie and Clyde, he is often remembered paradoxically as being a devoted family man who even had his wife and children on the run with him.

Public Enemies looks at the life and crime of the famous outlaw, but it also humanizes him and examines his lasting legacy. Along with pictures of Baby Face Nelson and important people, places, and events in his life, you will learn about the infamous public enemy like you never have before.

Bonnie Parker (1910-1934) and Clyde Barrow (1909-1934)

"You've read the story of Jesse James
Of how he lived and died
If you're still in need of something to read
Here's the story of Bonnie and Clyde." – Bonnie Parker, "The Trail's End"

There was no shortage of well known public enemies like John Dillinger and Baby Face Nelson, but none fascinated the American public as much as Bonnie and Clyde. While the duo and their Barrow Gang were no more murderous than other outlaws of the era, the duo's romantic relationship and the discovery of photographs at one of their hideouts added a more human dimension to Bonnie and Clyde, even as they were gunning down civilians and cops alike.

When Bonnie and Clyde were finally cornered and killed in a controversial encounter with police, a fate they shared with many other outlaws of the period, their reputations were cemented. In some way though, the sensationalized version of their life on the run is less interesting than reality, which included actual human drama within the gang.

Public Enemies looks at the lives and crimes of the famous outlaws, but it also humanizes them and examines their relationship. Along with pictures of Bonnie Parker, Clyde Barrow and important people, places, and events in their lives, you will learn about two of America's most notorious outlaws like you never have before.

Public Enemies: Al Capone, John Dillinger, Bonnie & Clyde, and Baby Face Nelson

About Charles River Editors

Introduction

Al Capone

    Chapter 1: The State of America in the Early 20th Century

        The Era of Progressive Reform

        Labor Strife and the "Red Scare"

        World War I and Its Aftermath

    Chapter 2: Capone's Early Years

        Roots in Naples

        Prejudice against Italian-Americans

        Capone's Childhood

        Capone Contracts Syphilis

        "Scarface"

        Marriage and Family

    Chapter 3: Prohibition

    Chapter 4: Capone's Rise to Power

        Chicago in 1920

        Torrio Consolidates Power

        Capone Settles In

        Expanding to the Suburbs

        Capone Loses a Brother

    Chapter 5: Gang Violence Erupts

        The "Beer Wars"

        Capone the Public Figure

        Massacre in New York

        A Public Official Is Murdered

        Capone Retreats, Then Returns

        Another Murder, Then Peace

        Capone Riding High

    Chapter 6: The Decline of Al Capone

        The Beginning of the End

        Capone's New Adversaries

        A Violent Start to 1928

- The St. Valentine's Day Massacre
- Capone Hides Out In Jail
- A New Decade, and a New World
- The Walls Close In
- Capone in Prison
- Chapter 7: The Man and the Myth

John Dillinger and Baby Face Nelson
- Chapter 1: Johnnie Dillinger
- Chapter 2: Young Lester Gillis
- Chapter 3: Dillinger's First Stint in Jail
- Chapter 4: Becoming Baby Face Nelson
- Chapter 5: Dillinger Becomes Famous
- Chapter 6: Dillinger and Baby Face Join Forces
- Chapter 7: The Battle of Barrington
- Chapter 8: The Dillinger Gang's Impact
- Bibliography

Bonnie & Clyde
- Chapter 1: A Girl Named Bonnie
- Chapter 2: A Boy Named Clyde
- Chapter 3: The Couple
- Chapter 4: The Barrow Gang
- Chapter 5: Celebrities
- Chapter 6: The Manhunt
- Chapter 7: Public Reaction
- Chapter 8: The Inevitable
- Chapter 9: The Legend of Bonnie and Clyde
- The Trail's End
- Suicide Sal
- Bibliography

Al Capone

Chapter 1: The State of America in the Early 20th Century

The early decades of the 20th century featured a series of growing pains for the United States as the nation entered a new century, a rapidly changing world, and a new stage in its own evolution. All at once, it seemed, American society was attempting to deal with the excesses and injustices of a rapidly industrializing and increasingly centralized economy, a wave of immigration changing the ethnic make-up of the country, and the emergence of new social movements fighting for causes like women's right to vote.

A driving political force during these years was the Progressive Movement, which on the one hand sought to ensure consumer and worker rights, and offset the growing power of big business. On the other hand, many backers of Progressivism were staunch capitalists intent on "rationalizing" capitalism to protect it from a possible threat posed by socialism, which, while much stronger in Europe, enjoyed considerable support in early 20th century America. Finally, Progressives echoed some of the moral concerns raised in the Third Great Awakening, a religious revival that swept America during the latter stages of the 1800s. Though the Progressive Movement began to dissipate during World War I, the Prohibition Act passed in 1919 and implemented in 1920 can be seen as Progressivism's last gasp.

It was on this contradictory stage—a nation with one foot in the 19th century and another in the 20th—that Al Capone famously and infamously strutted his stuff. He was the face of a multi-ethnic urban America, an early innovator in an almost corporate approach to organized crime, and a savvy manipulator of big-city politics. His mixture of sophistication and savagery mirrored that of a nation trying to harness its considerable but sometimes unruly energies. It was America's brief and disastrous attempt to outlaw the sale of alcohol—an experiment that in so many ways seemed at odds with a decade some have called The Roaring Twenties—that allowed Capone to garner the tremendous wealth and wield the outrageous power that made him an almost mythical, larger-than-life historical figure. And it was another of Progressivism's reforms, the establishment of a Federal Income Tax, which would in the end provide for Capone's downfall.

The Era of Progressive Reform

In the final decades of the 1800s, the United States was reshaped by the second wave of its Industrial Revolution, a fundamental economic transformation that included the building of transcontinental railroads, the explosive rise of the iron and steel industries, the birth of the automobile industry, and the widespread implementation of modernized factory production.

These changes produced great wealth and an improved quality of life for many, but considerable social upheaval as well. Traditional jobs on farms and in small trades were replaced by jobs in sweltering and often dangerous factories. Companies seeking competitive edge exploited underage and immigrant labor. The rapid growth of cities outpaced their ability to take care of the poor and disadvantaged.

In the early 1900s, a new generation of crusading journalists known as "muckrakers" campaigned to expose the social ills and abuses of power produced by unchecked capitalism. Their exposes resulted in reforms including child labor laws, the creation of the Food and Drug Administration, and the breaking up of the Standard Oil Company. Progressivism was less a movement than a set of ideals embraced by politicians from both major parties. Teddy Roosevelt, who took over the Presidency in 1901 after William McKinley's assassination and was reelected in a landslide in 1904, was one of the most prominent faces of Progressivism. He pushed for active enforcement of antitrust laws (proudly declaring himself a "trust-buster") and overall greater regulation of industry, and was an early voice for conservationism.

Progressives took up a variety of other causes, including civil service reforms to combat the power of big-city "machine" politics, as well as compulsory education laws. Though forward-looking in many ways, Progressivism was also nostalgic for the clearer morality of a bygone agrarian era, naively believing that government and industry could be made squeaky clean through the application of "scientific" principles. The support many Progressives lent to Prohibition reflects that naiveté.

Labor Strife and the "Red Scare"

With the exception of the IWW (International Workers of the World), organized labor was strongly supportive of the war effort, minimizing strikes and encouraging members to enlist. Union membership swelled during the war, and union leaders were hopeful that their wartime patriotism would be rewarded afterward. But a rocky and uneven economy led to an unprecedented number of strikes in 1919, as many as 3600 in total. Wartime unity was quickly forgotten as the government brought in troops to help quell a shipyard workers' strike in Seattle, a police strike in Boston, and later a series of strikes by steelworkers that resulted in the deaths of dozens of workers. Unions were charged with being "sovietism in disguise," and even President Wilson denounced the striking Boston police as "Bolsheviks."

The so-called "Red Scare" had its roots in wartime propaganda, and the government's insistence on "100% Americanism." But in the midst of the economic uncertainty and labor unrest that followed the war, "anti-Bolshevik" agitation only intensified. A series of unsuccessful bombings in early 1919 prompted Attorney General Palmer to create a new anti-radical division within the Justice Department's Bureau of Investigation (which in 1924 became the FBI). The head of the new division, J. Edgar Hoover, thus began a decades-long crusade against so-called "subversives." The Red Scare peaked later that year and early the next. In November 1919, Emma Goldman and 248 other radicals were deported and sent on a ship to the Soviet Union, and in a series of raids in January, as many as 6000 were arrested. But Palmer's warnings of a massive May Day uprising failed to materialize; and abroad, Bolshevism was contained in the Soviet Union and failed, as many had feared, to spread to Europe. Weary of conflict and politics, the American people embraced new President Warren Harding's "return to normalcy" and the Red Scare fizzled as quickly as it had flared up.

World War I and Its Aftermath

When war broke out in Europe in 1914, the United States was determined to maintain a neutral stance. Woodrow Wilson won the 1916 election on a platform of keeping the nation out of war. But German submarine attacks on British ships like the Lusitania (which resulted in hundreds of American deaths) finally prompted Congress to declare war on Germany in 1917. About 1.4 million men saw actual combat—53,000 of whom were killed, and over 200,000 injured. These numbers were high considering America's brief involvement in the war: the first U.S. troops arrived in June 1917, but didn't see significant action until the following spring. Within six months, the war was over. However, Allied troops remained in the area through 1920. The focus of their continued involvement was fear of the new Communist government in Russia (now the Soviet Union) that had overthrown the Czar in 1917, forcing Russia out of the war.

The war brought about a wide range of changes on the home front. President Wilson created a Committee on Public Information to generate wartime propaganda and instill patriotism. In its zeal to create unity at home, the government encouraged a backlash against immigrants, Germans especially, and branded all opposition to the war as "Bolshevism." Women were drafted into the wartime effort at home, and their participation created a heightened expectation for equal rights that helped lead to the 19th Amendment. The war also had a significant impact on black Americans. The closing off of immigration produced sudden labor shortages in Northern factories, prompting the initial stages of what is known as the Great Migration of black Americans from the South to the North. Also, the 400,000 black men who served in the military returned home with new hopes of a more equal footing in society. Finally, the extensive involvement of the government in the economy during the war, which included taking over the railroads, set the stage for a backlash against governmental intervention in the postwar years.

Chapter 2: Capone's Early Years

Young Al Capone with his mother

Roots in Naples

Although Al Capone will forever be associated with Chicago, he was a native Brooklyn tough with an unmistakable Italian background. Capone was not—as he often insisted, and as early accounts of his life claimed—born in Italy. His parents, Gabriele and Teresa, along with their first two children, arrived in New York in 1894, five years before Capone was born. They had come from Naples, a seaside city in the south of Italy, and the country's third largest. Naples was known for its long history of political instability, having fallen under the rule of a number of foreign powers, and also playing a role in the country's ongoing internal strife. Its government was weak, and into the political void stepped an organized crime syndicate called the Camorra, which infiltrated city government so thoroughly, especially the police department, that local officials sometimes turned to them to ensure public safety.

Chicago, the American city where Capone eventually ended up, was in many ways the American equivalent to Naples: a working-class, unruly and divided city that was a perfect breeding ground for organized crime. The parallels between how the Camorra operated in Naples and how Capone operated in Chicago are fascinating and undeniable, and it would be Capone who masterfully exploited them.[1]

Prejudice against Italian-Americans

The initial wave of Italian immigration in the late 1800s consisted mainly of single men

---

[1] Bergreen, *Capone*, p. 26

seeking to make some money and then return home to Italy, but Capone's parents were part of a new breed intent on staying and making a new life in the United States. There they indeed found opportunity, but also found themselves at the bottom of the ethnic pecking order. Italians were looked down on by most as the least desirable and least capable of the new immigrants. Even Jacob Riis, a crusading journalist and social reformer who exposed the appalling conditions of immigrants in his famous book *How the Other Half Lives,* concurred with this assessment: "The Italian comes in at the bottom... and stays there."[2]

Making matters even worse, among Italian immigrants, those from Southern Italy were viewed as the lowest of the low. Indeed, even back in Italy, Southern Italians had been the object of the scorn of their Northern countrymen. At the same time, this shared prejudice didn't exactly bring Capone and other Italian-Americans with roots in Naples closer to their Sicilian compatriots. Throughout his life, Capone would distance himself from, and find himself at odds with, Sicilian organized crime leaders.

Capone's Childhood

Capone's early years in New York were certainly not easy ones, but his childhood was hardly one of destitution. His father was a barber who eventually came to own his own shop, and the family moved around in Brooklyn through a series of progressively nicer apartments. Neighbors later remembered the family as quiet and respectable. Capone for his part was a solid B-student through the fifth grade, and though he was involved in the occasional neighborhood scuffle, he was not an especially troublesome child.

The following year, however, young Alphonse reached a turning point. Al started missing school and was asked to repeat the 6th grade. When a teacher reprimanded him for misconduct and struck him (not unusual at the time), the boy struck back and was expelled. Still in his early teens, young Al Capone never returned to school. Yet even this early rebellion was not remarkable, and it didn't inevitably mark the young Capone for a life of crime. In fact, it was unusual for immigrant children to move on to high school anyway.

It was where Al decided to start hanging out that set him down his notorious path. Young Al began spending a good part of his days at a local pool hall and became quite proficient at the game. Just down the street was the headquarters of Johnny Torrio, a local racketeer who would later take Capone under his wings and become Scarface's most important mentor. Al started out running small errands for Torrio, and it was in these early stages that he proved himself to be reliable and trustworthy.

---

[2] quoted in Bergreen, *Capone,* p. 22

Giovanni "Johnny" Torrio

As he grew older, Capone occasionally flirted with local gang activity, but otherwise appeared headed on a respectable if unremarkable path. He worked for three years at a munitions factory, and later as a paper cutter. The adolescent Capone enjoyed dressing up and going out, but didn't especially stand out from others. The novelist Daniel Fuchs remembered him as "something of a nonentity, affable, soft of speech and even mediocre in everything but dancing."[3]

Though Capone's time at clubs like the Broadway Casino was innocent enough, he also began hanging out at the Adonis Social Club, which attracted a more volatile crowd. It was in the Adonis basement, where guests were known to engage in target practice shooting at beer bottles, that Al learned how to handle a revolver and likely developed a taste for the kind of crowd he would later run with.

Capone Contracts Syphilis

It wasn't unusual for young men like Capone to find their first sexual encounters among the local prostitutes, and it is almost certain that it was around this time that Al contracted syphilis. Awareness of venereal disease was only just beginning to take hold among public health officials, triggered in part by screenings during the war-time draft in which 10% of the young men tested positive.

Syphilis (whose origins can be traced, ironically, to Naples) has three distinct stages. The first two are relatively benign and consist of genital sores and then flu-like symptoms, both of which usually go away on their own. Among an unlucky 20%, the disease then goes into an extended latent phase, its later third stage subtle but deadly, and often undiagnosed because its victims have long assumed the disease went away on its own. The third stage attacks the frontal lobe of

---

[3] Bergreen, *Capone*, p. 43

the brain in somewhat the same ways as Alzheimer's, but gradually and over many years. It eventually results in dementia, but long before that produces a series of personality changes and distortions that include irritability, sudden mood swings, and megalomania. Though Capone's symptoms didn't become glaring until much later, recent biographers credit the disease with playing a central role in Al's transformation from an unremarkable youth only occasionally caught up in trouble to a volatile and feared ringleader of organized crime. The disease would also be blamed for Capone's later descent into dementia near the end of his life.

"Scarface"

It was under the influence of local racketeer Johnny Torrio that young Al Capone began veering from any semblance of a life of respectability. One of Torrio's associates, the gangster and hitman Frankie Yale, had just opened a bar on Coney Island he called the Harvard Club (though it was hardly an Ivy League-type establishment). He needed someone who could double as a bartender and bouncer, and Torrio recommended the 17 year old Capone. Yale and Capone hit it off, and Al became a fixture at the new club.

Frankie Yale

A year into his tenure, Al was waiting a table and in a lapse of judgment made a suggestive remark about a young lady seated there. Her brother, drunk and outraged, leapt up in her defense and in the scuffle that followed ended up slashing Capone several times across the face with a knife. Though there was a good deal of blood, the damage was not serious, but the scars remained visible for the rest of Capone's life, and he was greatly self-conscious and vain about them. He concocted cover stories that included one about the scars being a war injury, even though he never served. He even went so far as to cover them up with make-up, and insisted on being photographed on the side where the scars didn't show. He hated his unofficial (and still best known) nickname "Scarface," preferring "Snorky," slang at the time for someone who was a stylish dresser.

Capone's very visible scars on his left cheek

Despite that incident, Capone's standing with Frankie Yale was such that he was allowed to stay on at the Harvard Club, and Capone even subsequently used his attacker, Frank Gallucio, as a bodyguard. Moreover, his duties were expanded to include helping his boss collect on unpaid debts, a task that in 1919 led to a far more serious of act of violence when Al ended up shooting a man who wouldn't pay up on a gambling debt. This, too, ended up becoming part of the Capone legend: that he shortly after fled to Chicago to escape a murder rap. But in fact Al's path to Chicago and a full-time life of organized crime was not so direct.

Marriage and Family

Around this same time, Al began looking for more lasting romantic companionship. He became smitten with a free-spirited Italian girl just down the street, but apparently her parents didn't find Capone to be a suitable match, so he began searching elsewhere. At a club further away where the Italian neighborhood bordered the Irish, he met a quiet Irish girl named Mary Coughlin. At first glance, this seemed like an odd match, since she was not Italian and came from a solid midd-class family. But despite these very obvious differences, she was instantly smitten with Al, and she would remain devoted to him the rest of their life together in spite of his criminal activities and frequent womanizing.

Mae Capone

It wasn't long before Mae, as she was known, became pregnant, giving birth to their first child, Sonny, in early December of 1918. As a young child, Sonny suffered from frequent infections and loss of hearing, likely a result of Capone's syphilis. It wasn't until later that month that the couple actually married, a wedding that occurred at least in part so Al could avoid the draft.

Now a family man, Capone once more set himself on a path of respectability, not only leaving Frankie Yale and the Harvard Club, but deciding his youthful stomping grounds might not make the best place to raise a family. In early 1920 he relocated to Baltimore and found work as a bookkeeper for a construction company, where he displayed solid accounting skills and a good head for numbers. But no sooner had he established his new life when his father suddenly passed away later that year. Al's oldest brother had shipped out west, and the next youngest, Ralph, was in no position to take responsibility for the widowed Teresa and the three younger children.

While back in town for the funeral, Al resumed contact with Johnny Torrio, who around this time had decided that Prohibition-era Chicago was where the real money could be made, and he had already begun working for the city's top organized crime figure. Torrio persuaded his young protégé to follow him, and in early 1921 Capone gave his notice to the construction firm and headed west.[4]

Chapter 3: Prohibition

Though Prohibition was ultimately a poorly conceived and poorly implemented disaster, it is not as simple a story as it might first appear to be. The Temperance Movement, as it was first known, dated all the way back to the 1840s, when drinking was an undeniable problem in American life. Historians estimate that per capita consumption of booze was as high as 7 gallons of pure alcohol a year, well over three times the current rate, and the equivalent of 90 bottles of 80-proof liquor a year. In response to this very real problem, groups like the Daughters of Temperance began cropping up, and later the Women's Christian Temperance Union. The Prohibition Party was founded in 1872, but it was the Anti-Saloon League, founded in 1893, that made prohibition a viable political force.

Temperance was connected in unexpected ways to a variety of other causes. The WCTU was at the center of the women's suffrage movement: it provided a training ground for women in political activism, and women concerned about moral issues like drinking realized they would have greater impact if given the right to vote. Most prominent abolitionists were in favor of temperance, as were prominent black leaders like Frederick Douglass and Booker T. Washington. Prohibition also attracted activists of a very different sort: beer and saloons were very much associated with the new wave of immigration, and the ASL in particular had a strongly anti-immigrant bent. Thus, the politics of the temperance movement was all over the map, and made for strange and contradictory alliances.

Prohibition also came to be connected with the campaign for a federal income tax. The alcohol excise tax accounted for a substantial amount of the government's budget, forcing supporters of Prohibition to answer the question of how to replace that income, and thus creating additional momentum for the 16th Amendment approved in 1913. And conversely, the need to bolster the federal budget in the early days of the Depression became one of many reasons cited for Prohibition's repeal.

Passing Prohibition was one thing, but enforcing it was another, and in many ways Prohibition seemed doomed from the start. The new Prohibition Bureau was a part of the Treasury Department, whose head, Andrew Mellon, never fully supported the law. The Bureau was given only 1500 field agents to start with, and much of the hiring of agents was influenced by the Anti-Saloon League, which used the positions to pay back political favors from the Prohibition campaign. In a fascinating historical footnote, it turns out Capone's eldest brother, who had

---

[4] Bergreen, p. 58

earlier moved out West and disappeared from sight, reinvented himself under a new name and became a well-known and highly regarded Prohibition Agent. He eventually reconnected with his family, visiting them yearly in Chicago and largely managing to keep his two lives separate.

The ways of circumventing Prohibition were many and varied. Whiskey and gin and rum were smuggled in through Canada and the Bahamas, among other places. A line of ships along the East Coast permanently docked just beyond the three-mile border, and essentially serving as liquor warehouses, was known as Rum Row. Doctors were allowed to write prescriptions for "medicinal" alcohol, and exemptions for wine designated for Communion were available. In addition to all the money to be made from outright bootlegging, apparently legitimate businesses thrived as well: for example, the number of Walgreens pharmacies shot up from 20 to 525 over the course of the 1920s. Foreign travel shot up, and ship lines developed "cruises to nowhere" or "booze cruises."

Disenchantment with Prohibition grew steadily as the decade progressed. So-called "dry" crusaders didn't help their cause with overly zealous measures like the Jones Law, which aimed to make all violations of Prohibition a felony. But it was the stock market crash and the Depression that was the nail in the coffin for Prohibition. Voters were disillusioned with the Republican Party, and in the 1932 election FDR argued that the government desperately needed the income from alcohol taxes. To a large extent that was accurate; during the first year of Repeal, such taxes accounted for 9% of all federal revenue. In February 1933, the 21st Amendment (repealing the 18th) was introduced, and when in December the necessary number of states had ratified it, Prohibition's 14 year history was over.

Among Prohibition's long-term (and unintended) consequences was the nationalization of organized crime. The complex transportation schemes required to move liquor like Canadian whiskey across the border, then to New York, and then on to Chicago also fostered the creation of regional and national networks among racketeers and bootleggers. Organized crime became organized and bureaucratized as never before. As historian Selwyn Raab wrote in *The Five Families,* "Prohibition had been the catalyst for transforming the neighborhood gangs of the 1920s into smoothly run regional and national criminal corporations... Bootlegging gave them on-the-job executive training."[5]

Chapter 4: Capone's Rise to Power

Chicago in 1920

Founded in 1832, and through the mid-1800s a largely provincial regional hub, Chicago was rebuilt after the Great Fire of 1871 as a modern city made of steel and iron and granite. By 1920 its population was nearly 3 million, the second largest in the country, and it was the undisputed

---

[5] quoted in Okrent, *Last Call,* p. 345

capital of mid-America. Dominated economically by industries like meatpacking, lumber and the railroads, Chicago was a richly diverse and heavily segregated city.

Lacking the established elite and long-standing cultural traditions of eastern cities like New York and Boston, Chicago was notable for its loose and open nature. It was a city in which an ambitious businessman (or gangster) could make an almost immediate impact. In the eyes of many, its looseness extended to matters of morality as well. In his 1904 book *The Shame of the Cities,* muckraking journalist Lincoln Steffens summed the city up this way: "First in violence, deepest in dirt; loud, lawless, unlovely, ill-smelling, irreverent… the 'tough' among cities, a spectacle for the nation."[6]

Torrio Consolidates Power

Johnny Torrio was summoned to Chicago to be the right-hand man for James "Big Jim" Colosimo, who had emerged from the post-war years as the leader of the city's most prominent organized crime syndicate. Colosimo lived large and extravagantly, and he saw the business-like and unassuming Torrio as a perfect match. The cornerstone of Colosimo's expanding empire was a large network of brothels, and the new Prohibition laws provided yet another possibility for growth. Even before this expansion, Colosimo came into frequent conflict with the Black Hand, which had prompted his association with Torrio in the first place. When Torrio first introduced Capone to Chicago, Capone worked as a bouncer and bartender at one of Colosimo's brothels, the Four Deuces.

However, Torrio's arrival on the scene happened to coincide with Colosimo's rapid and unexpected demise. Big Jim fell fast and hard for a young actress and singer, and rashly divorced his wife and former business partner, leaving the day-to-day operations almost entirely to Torrio. Because of this, as well as his reluctance to engage in liquor smuggling, Colosimo was increasingly perceived as vulnerable, a situation that was quickly taken advantage of by Torrio. When Big Jim returned to Chicago after his recent second marriage, Torrio called him to let him know that a shipment was arriving at his café. When Colosimo showed up at the café to get the package, he was shot and killed.

Though nobody was ever convicted, it has long been assumed that Colosimo's assassin was none other than Frankie Yale, Torrio's and Capone's old associate back in New York. By this time Yale had established himself as one of the most prominent gangsters in New York City, but perhaps jealous of Torrio's new success in Chicago and wishing to make his own mark, Yale travelled to Chicago and on May 11, 1920 he allegedly took out Colosimo in the first of many notorious gangland hits to come. Yale was picked up after an eyewitness identified him, but he was later released when the witness claimed his memory had failed him. Capone himself also

---

[6] Bergreen, p. 77

continues to be a suspected assassin of Big Jim.

Big Jim Colosimo

Big Jim may have been going soft, but he had done a credible job of organizing a criminal syndicate, and regardless of who murdered Big Jim, the political climate in Chicago was a perfect setting for Torrio to establish himself in the wake of Colosimo's killing. New mayor "Big Bill" Thompson openly promised to turn a blind eye to the Prohibition laws—declaring that Chicago was "wet," and so was he. Torrio quickly ingratiated himself with the Thompson administration and began expanding the network he inherited from Colosimo, as well as establishing peace with a number of the many other crime syndicates in the city. It wasn't long before his operation included thousands of speakeasies, brothels, and gambling joints. Torrio needed some men he could trust to help him run his new empire, and it was at that point that he turned to his 22 year old protégé Al Capone.

Mayor "Big Bill" Thompson

Capone Settles In

Capone initially moved out on his own, followed shortly by older brother Ralph, and the two started out managing a handful of brothels for Torrio. Capone's other older brother, Frank, also moved out and joined the Torrio operation. Less than a year later, Al was named manager of the Four Deuces, a saloon and gambling den that served as the headquarters of Torrio's empire. It was a significant promotion, and Al was now put on a salary. Showing his growing business savvy, Capone set up a couple of front businesses—one identifying him as a second-hand furniture dealer, as well as a second office opened under the alias "A. Brown, MD" complete with a waiting room with bottles of legal medicinal alcohol on display.

Ralph "Bottles" Capone

With his wife and son still back in Brooklyn, Al lived the high life and started to get carried away. Driving drunk one night, he crashed into a parked taxi and, irrationally enraged at the cabbie, pulled a gun on him and flashed a fake sheriff's badge. The incident resulted in the first of Capone's arrests, followed just as quickly by his quiet release after Torrio pulled the necessary strings. Later that year, in 1922, Al had enough money to buy a nice home on a quiet street, and he soon sent for his wife and son, as well as his widowed mother, younger brothers, and sister. Capone reestablished a lower profile, and for several years no one in the neighborhood suspected he was anything but a respectable businessman.

Expanding to the Suburbs

After eight scandal-ridden years in office, the permissive "Big Bill" Thompson was finally forced to withdraw from the 1923 mayoral election, and his successor, William Dever, vowed to make a radical change in direction—not only enforcing Prohibition, but cracking down on organized crime. The new policy heightened tension between the various gangs competing for a share of all the illegal profits to be had in Chicago, and it brought about the early stages of a long series of turf wars in the city.

Mayor William Dever

Torrio's response was to keep a low profile in Chicago itself and shift the focus of operations to the suburbs. Thus, Torrio and Capone chose Cicero, a sleepy working-class suburb whose residents loved their beer but were more conservative when it came to vices like prostitution. In late 1923, Torrio set up the first two of many brothels to come, established a profit-sharing arrangement with rival gangs, and then left Capone in charge while he took some time off to move his aging mother back to Italy. In an effort spearheaded by older brother Frank—who with his tall good looks was the most publicly visible of the Capone brothers—the Capones began a systematic effort to take control of Cicero's political establishment. They put up their own candidates, intimidated the opposition, and stole ballot boxes, whatever it took: and sure enough, the Capone-backed candidates were swept into office by wide margins.

With Cicero's City Hall in his back pocket, Capone and his brothers engaged in aggressive expansion, establishing a large new brothel in the neighboring suburb of Forest View (which came to be called "Caponeville"), a major new gambling hall, and taking over the local racetrack. The only opposition the brothers encountered came from the local paper, the *Cicero Tribune,* run by a high-minded journalist named Robert St. John.

Capone Loses a Brother

As the political primaries of 1924 approached, the stream of critical coverage from St. John finally had an effect. The far more influential *Chicago Tribune* picked up the story, predicting intimidation and violence in the upcoming elections, and a crusading judge convinced Mayor Dever to let him deputize members of the Chicago police force, who otherwise had no jurisdiction in Cicero, to monitor the elections and ensure peace. The plan backfired as the fleet of 70 cops arrived in plain clothes and in unmarked black sedans similar to those used by the Capones and other gangs. When Frank Capone saw a long line of black cars arrive and the non-uniformed police began to get out, he assumed they represented a rival gang, reached for his gun and was mowed down by the police, who fired dozens of shots. Though the police would later claim Frank fired at the officers first, other bystanders claimed Frank did nothing more than reach for his gun. On April 4, 1924, Frank was given a quintessential mob funeral, replete with $20,000 worth of flowers (ironically bought from one of Capone's gangster rivals, Dion O'Banion) and a huge motorcade.

A grief-stricken Al was now more determined than ever to ruthlessly acquire and exercise power. Only Torrio, back from Italy, convinced him not to declare war on the Chicago police. Nevertheless, Capone's rage spilled over five weeks after the funeral when his good friend Jack Guzik was insulted by a small-time hoodlum, for which Capone sought out and killed the man. As would happen again and again, several eyewitnesses to the shooting suddenly developed a case of poor memory, and despite a state attorney's best efforts to indict Capone, no charges were ever filed.

Chapter 5: Gang Violence Erupts

The "Beer Wars"

Although Torrio tried to maintain the peace among Chicago's many racketeers and organized crime syndicates, turf battles in what the press called the "Beer Wars" began breaking out and escalating. So-called "gangland-style" murders rose from 29 in 1922 to 52 in 1923. One of the major players in the war—the Irish gangster Dion O'Banion, the most prominent organized crime figure on the North Side—made a small fortune through the flower shop he ran as his front business: it became accepted practice, even for rival gangs, to order flowers for the constant stream of gang funerals through his shop.

O'Banion

The other major players in the Beer Wars were the six Genna brothers, a tough and volatile group of Sicilian bootleggers. Torrio and Capone maintained an uneasy peace with them, but tension ran high between the Gennas and O'Banion and ultimately full-scale war broke out. O'Banion highjacked one of the Gennas' trucks, and then in an ambitious double-crossing scheme leaked a tip to the police that set up Torrio and Capone to be arrested at a brewery the three of them jointly owned. Capone escaped, but Torrio did not. Though he was soon out on bail, even Torrio gave up on keeping the peace, and in November of 1924 he and Capone teamed up with the Genna brothers and arranged a dramatic slaying of O'Banion in his own flower shop. For the hit, Torrio and Capone relied on an old acquaintance: none other than Frankie Yale. When Yale entered O'Banion's flower shop with gunmen John Scalise and Albert Anselmi, O'Banion recognized him and greeted him with a handshake. Yale then held onto O'Banion's hand while Scalise and Anselmi fired bullets into O'Banion's chest, cheeks, and throat, killing him on the spot.

The murder of O'Banion only heightened the now burgeoning gang war between the hoods on the North Side and the Torrio/Capone syndicate on the South Side. The violence continued unabated as O'Banion's allies—including "Hymie" Weiss and "Bugs" Moran—fought to hold onto O'Banion's North Side turf and exact revenge for his murder. Still facing charges and an inevitable trial, Torrio exited the scene for Hot Springs, Arkansas, again leaving Capone in charge. Knowing he was a target, Al took heightened security measures, but even still he just narrowly escaped an assassination attempt by Weiss, Moran, and Vincent "The Schemer" Drucci on January 25, 1925, who riddled Capone's car. The failed attack featured a new weapon on the Chicago gang scene: the Thompson submachine gun, or "tommy gun" as it would popularly be known. Capone quickly acquired his own arsenal, and the Beer Wars took on a new savagery.

Hymie Weiss

Bugs Moran

Two days later, Torrio was himself the object of an assassination attempt. As Torrio was heading toward his apartment after shopping with his wife, Weiss, Moran and Vincent Drucci poured gunfire into Torrio's car, hitting him in the jaw, lungs, groin, legs, and abdomen. Moran walked up to finish Torrio off with a shot to the head but had run out of ammunition, and the three assailants fled before making sure Torrio was dead. Somehow, the severely wounded Torrio managed to survive, spending weeks recovering in the hospital, with Capone providing protection around the clock. He healed only to have to finally face the federal charges that came out of the brewery raid. Though convicted and sentenced to serve nine months, the wounded Torrio pulled the necessary strings and had an easy time of it in jail in a well-furnished private cell. Upon being released, he announced his retirement and was spirited away to New York. Happy to make it out alive, Torrio told Capone, "It's all yours Al. Me? I'm quitting. It's Europe for me."

Capone was now fully in charge of the Chicago Outfit

Vincent "The Schemer" Drucci

Capone the Public Figure

Despite his rapid rise to power, Al Capone had until now largely stayed out of the public eye. A number of media stories following Frank's murder failed, in fact, to even get his name right. But upon assuming control of Torrio's organization in the spring of 1925, Capone relocated the center of his operations to a high-profile hotel, the Metropole, and made a new effort to enter and remain in the limelight. He carefully fashioned a public image, not as a gangster, but as a well-dressed, charismatic businessman. He became close friends with the journalist Harry Read, who helped school Capone on his public image, and Capone began appearing at public events like baseball games. He even made almost daily visits to City Hall, and though he had no interest in public office, he carried himself like an elected official.

Capone undeniably struck an impressive public figure. Already very wealthy, Capone traveled in style, frequently wearing custom suits, chomping on cigars, enjoying good food and drink, and frequently accompanied by women. Clearly a celebrity, he and the media relished each other, and it was through the media that Capone delivered the classic quotes he was known for: "I am just a businessman, giving the people what they want," and "All I do is satisfy a public demand."

Of course, nobody was more aware than Capone what kind of danger he was actually in. Hand-in-hand with his new public visibility, Capone implemented a series of extravagant security measures. His new headquarters at the Metropole included a network of tunnels originally built for hauling coal but now refurbished as alternate exits. He traveled in a customized armored Cadillac sedan that weighed seven tons and was always accompanied by a convoy of bodyguards. "Hymie" Weiss and "Bugs" Moran were still bitter over O'Banion's murder and had one by one picked off several of the Genna brothers. Capone figured sooner or later they would come after him again.

Massacre in New York

In late 1925, Al Capone took a trip back east with a highly personal agenda, but also a business one. The personal agenda concerned an emergency operation for his son Sonny, who continued to suffer from a variety of health problems. Back east, Capone sought the best treatment money could buy, and got it. With Sonny's operation a success, Capone took care of some business in New York, meeting with his old associate Frankie Yale to establish a pipeline for bootlegging Canadian whiskey through New York and then on to Chicago. Their business complete, Frankie offered to host a Christmas night celebration at one of his old haunts, the Adonis Social Club, with Al as his honored guest.

Brooklyn at that time was in the midst of its own gang war, with Yale and the Italians against Richard Lonergan and the Irish. Yale received a tip the night before that Lonergan was going to target the party, and his first instinct was to cancel the celebration. But Capone glimpsed an opportunity and arranged an ambush. A fierce gun battle took place inside the club, killing Lonergan and three of his associates. In one bloody Christmas night, Capone had strengthened his alliance with Yale, put his fellow Italians in charge of Brooklyn, and established Chicago as the new center of power in organized crime.

But is that how it actually went down? Some have claimed that this is another embellished tale in the legend of Al Capone. According to author Patrick Downey, the killing of Lonergan and his associates at the Adonis Club was not an ambush but more likely an unplanned, spur of the moment shooting that came about in response to a drunken argument between Capone and Lonergan's associate, Needles Ferry. Witnesses also reported Lonergan and his crew were heavily intoxicated and shouting ethnic slurs at bar patrons. However, according to reports, when police found Ferry and Lonergan, they'd been shot execution style.

A Public Official Is Murdered

Chicago had seen its share of notorious murders over the course of the 1920s, but the killing of an assistant state attorney in the spring of 1926 truly shocked a city that wasn't easily shocked, and it triggered a crisis that would ultimately discredit city and state officials alike.

In a bizarre night that would take months for authorities to unravel, William McSwiggin, the attorney who had tried to indict Capone for murder back in 1924, got caught up in a Cicero turf war between Capone and two rival bootleggers, the O'Donnell brothers. While maintaining a tough-on-crime public image, privately McSwiggin had made accommodations with a number of gangsters, including Capone. With a penchant for vice as a card player, gambler, and drinker, McSwiggin naturally came into contact with and even befriended Al Capone.

On this night in 1926, however, McSwiggin chanced into meeting up with the O'Donnells after he had been out drinking and his car broke down. That same night, the brothers made a fateful decision to go cruising in Cicero, and the group made their way to the Pony Inn, a Capone-run speakeasy near Capone's headquarters in Cicero. Capone got word that the O'Donnells' Lincoln had been spotted cruising his territory, interpreted this as a provocation, and had the group (which also included the sons of two cops) gunned down as they exited a local bar.

As fate would have it, the O'Donnells escaped, but McSwiggin and the two young men were killed. While Capone went into hiding, the city was in an uproar over the killing of a well-known prosecutor whose seedy connections were a mystery known only amongst his associates. The newspapers were full of speculation, and McSwiggin's boss, state attorney Robert Crowe, publicly declared his belief that Capone was behind the murder. He deputized 300 detectives who scoured Cicero and Chicago, looking for clues. Over the course of six months, six separate grand juries were convened, but no indictment was ever handed down. Powerless to find or indict Al, public officials began a campaign of harassment targeting various Capone businesses—all of which simply underscored the futility of the high-profile investigation.

Capone would never enjoy the public immunity he had owned in previous years.

Capone Retreats, Then Returns

Remarkably, Capone remained at large for nearly four months—initially hiding out with friends in the outlying community of Chicago Heights. He then put even more distance between himself and Chicago, retreating 200 miles away to Lansing, Michigan, home to a vibrant Italian-American community, a number of whom had relocated from Chicago. At first keeping a very low profile near a lake outside of Lansing, Capone over the months came out of the shadows and became a visible if discreet presence in Lansing—well-known in the Italian community, and even among public officials and police. Those who knew him during this period invariably describe him as well-dressed, polite, and generous with the community. It appears he took stock of his life at this point, and made a decision to try to reinvent himself as a respectable businessman.

Knowing he couldn't run forever, Capone began a series of unofficial long-distance negotiations with Chicago law enforcement, and in late July of 1926 returned to Chicago and turned himself in. It was a risky move, and Capone casually asserted his innocence to anyone who would listen, describing the murdered McSwiggin as a friend, and even bragging that he was on the Capone payroll. The gamble paid off when the judge quickly dismissed the case for lack of evidence.

Capone was back in business.

Another Murder, Then Peace

While Capone was intent on attaining respectability and distancing himself from his image as a gangster, the longstanding feud with Hymie Weiss continued to fester. The two sides traded attacks, with Capone miraculously escaping a spectacular armed assault on the Hawthorne Hotel in Cicero. On September 20, 1926, North Side gang assailants riding in a motorcade of ten vehicles sprayed gunfire from tommy guns and shotguns at Capone while he was dining in a restaurant on the first floor. Capone was saved by bodyguard, Frankie Rio, who threw him to the ground immediately, but bullets and flying glass injured many innocent bystanders. Since he was the target, Capone paid for the medical care of some of the victims, and shaken by the nearly successful attempt, which he correctly assumed was the work of the North Side, he decided to attempt to negotiate a truce.

Despite Capone's entreaties, Bugs Moran and Hymie Weiss would have none of it unless Capone had John Scalise and Albert Anselmi (who were responsible for Dion O'Banion's hit) killed. Thus, Capone concocted a fool-proof plan. At 4:00 on the afternoon of October 11, 1926, Hymie Weiss and some of his men headed for their headquarters, the old Schofield flower shop. After parking their cars and walking toward the building, two gunmen who were hidden nearby opened fire on the group with a submachine gun and a shotgun, mortally wounding Weiss and killing one of his associates. There was considerable speculation about Capone's role in the killing, but no charges were filed. Capone had just eliminated one of his mortal enemies.

With Weiss out of the picture, Capone made another bold and audacious move: hosting a "peace conference" designed to produce a lasting peace between Chicago's rival gangs. In classic Capone style, he made no attempt to disguise the nature of the meeting or its participants, and held it in full public view at a hotel near City Hall and across the street from the office of the chief of police. Former Mayor "Big Bill" Thompson, seeking a political comeback, was asked to preside and accepted. The meeting was a success and a "general amnesty" was agreed upon. For 70 days afterward, there wasn't a single murder connected with bootlegging, the longest stretch of peace since the start of Prohibition. Publicly, Capone even spoke of retiring.

Capone Riding High

Discredited by the fiasco of the McSwiggin investigation, William Dever was ousted from the mayor's office and replaced in early 1927 by his old foe "Big Bill" Thompson. With the amiable and lax Thompson back in office, Capone emerged from his unofficial retirement and assumed a more visible public role than ever. His headquarters at the Metropole expanded to fifty rooms, nearly the entire hotel, and was the site of non-stop drinking and gambling and prostitution. Capone was seen prominently at a wide range of sporting events, especially Cubs games, and was a member of the official delegation greeting Charles Lindbergh after his successful transatlantic flight. He hosted a huge public party following the much-anticipated heavyweight rematch between Jack Dempsey and Gene Tunney, and he even conducted the band he had hired as it played Gershwin's "Rhapsody in Blue."

The year 1927 saw the Capone organization's income hit new highs—over $100 million by some estimates. A brief stretch of violence broke out as Capone skirmished with an up-and-coming rival, Joseph Aiello, trying to move in on the always hotly contested North Side territory. But a few months later, fearing for his life, Aiello and his two brothers fled town. Capone held a press conference and brazenly announced, "I'm the boss. I'm going to continue to run things."[7]

Aiello

Chapter 6: The Decline of Al Capone

The Beginning of the End

Though Al Capone appeared to be on top of the world at the close of 1927, the elements of his downfall were starting to fall into place. While Chicago Mayor "Big Bill" Thompson was content to look the other way, a new breed of law enforcement officials had no such patience for

---
[7] Bergreen, p. 239

business as usual. Among these was a new chief of police, Mike Hughes, who promised a crackdown on gangs and hundreds of new cops on the street. Angered by this new policy, and not trusting or respecting Thompson, Capone impulsively announced he was retiring from the Chicago scene—and this time seemed to really mean it. In a long, rambling, self-pitying monologue to the press, Capone declared he was heading to Florida at the end of the year. "Let the worthy citizens of Chicago get their liquor the best they can. I'm sick of the job. It's a thankless one and full of grief."[8]

In early December, Capone indeed boarded a train—but for Los Angeles and not Florida. Much to his surprise, he was treated coldly there. The chief of police told him he was not welcome and gave him 12 hours to leave. Though he ended up staying a few days longer, Capone was soon back on a train to Illinois. Back in Chicago, Hughes had announced an ambitious plan to put all gangsters under arrest. Capone got off the train early, in Joliet, only to be arrested there and quickly released.

Soon after New Year's, Capone finally did head to Florida, to the city of Miami. Though public officials there also expressed mixed feelings about Capone's presence, the city, which had been devastated by a hurricane the previous year, was badly in need of new investment, and privately the mayor arranged for Capone to buy an expensive villa on Palm Island through an intermediary. As hard as he fought for social respectability in Miami, it continually eluded him. The details of his real estate transaction eventually were made public, and though Capone and later his wife remained in the villa for years (after spending most of the 1930s in jail, Capone would return there to die), he was never truly accepted, and his presence there was always considered an embarrassment.

Capone's New Adversaries

Though the new Chicago chief of police succeeded at times in making life difficult for Capone, it was three other officials who were ultimately instrumental in bringing him down. The most famous was Eliot Ness, a Treasury agent later hired to work for the Chicago Prohibition Bureau. Ness conducted a series of dramatic raids targeting Capone's bootlegging operation—a story he captured with considerable embellishment in his book *The Untouchables,* later made into both a TV series and a movie.

---

[8] Bergreen, p. 262

Elliot Ness

Ness is best remembered as the man most responsible for bringing Capone down, but in fact it was U.S. Attorney George Johnson, the man who hired Ness for the Chicago office, who played a more substantial role in Capone's demise. He saw to it that, for the first time, various agencies coordinated their efforts against Capone at a high level. Perhaps just as important, and working almost entirely out of the limelight, was Treasury Department investigator Frank Wilson, who worked tirelessly for years to compile a case against Capone for tax evasion. More worried about the various murder raps he was associated with, Capone never took the tax evasion charges seriously until it was too late.

A Violent Start to 1928

"Big Bill" Thompson's second stay in the mayor's office was just as disastrous as his first. His negligence and incompetence gave organized crime free reign for a while, but it also led to political instability. As an important primary approached in April (one widely viewed as a referendum on his administration), the city was rocked by a series of bombings targeting public officials. With Capone spending much of his time in Miami, there was no one to enforce the peace, and freelancers looking to establish their clout were likely responsible. Election Day itself was a violent and often chaotic affair, but the voters nonetheless rejected many of Thompson's men. Thompson, who had been harboring ambitions for a presidential campaign, began to show less and less interest in the city's daily affairs.

In 1927, Capone had begun to suspect that his old associate (and former boss at the Harvard

Club) Frankie Yale was orchestrating hijackings of his own whiskey shipments and then keeping the booze for himself. Capone asked James "Filesy" DeAmato, an old friend, to get to the bottom of things, and DeAmato confirmed Capone's suspicions, reporting that Frankie was hijacking the booze shipments. Shortly after that, DeAmato's cover was blown, leading him to attempt a haphazard attempt on Frankie Yale's life on the night of July 1, 1927. That attempt failed, but the hit on Filesy DeAmato six nights later did not, as DeAmato was gunned down on a Brooklyn street corner.

DeAmato may have failed to kill Yale, but Capone was a bit more experienced in that regard, and when he returned to Miami the next month, Capone began making plans to have Yale assassinated. On July 1, 1928, a year to the date of DeAmato's attempt on his life, Yale received a phone call at one of his clubs informing him that something was wrong with his wife Lucy, who at the time Yale assumed was at home caring for their infant daughter. Not thinking clearly, Yale quickly jumped into his car and sped off, only to notice at a red light that he was being tailed by a Buick with four passengers. After a chase up New Utrecht and onto 44th Street, the Buick's passengers riddled Yale's car with shotguns and submachine guns. Yale's car was outfitted with armor, but his windows were not bullet-proof. Laying dead in his car on a Brooklyn street corner, Yale was wearing a luxurious belt buckle believed to have been given him by Al Capone.

Yale received a huge, opulent funeral with some 100,000 attendees, a reflection of Yale's huge status in the racketeering world. While Yale's gangland funeral set the gold standard for mob funerals, it did not include Capone, who had carefully arranged to be in Miami at the time. Though Capone was never formally connected to Yale's murder, the presence of cars with Chicago plates at the scene of the crime inevitably drew suspicion his way, and the use of tommy guns was a hallmark of Chicago gangland warfare that had previously not been used in New York City. In later years, researchers concluded that Yale's assassins included Capone gunmen Fred "Killer" Burke, Gus Winkler, George "Shotgun" Ziegler, and Louis "Little New York" Campagna, most of whom would participate in the St. Valentine's Day Massacre seven months later. Furthermore, one of the tommy guns used in the St. Valentine's Day Massacre would later be linked by ballistic testing to Yale's murder.

To all outward appearances, Capone was still on top. Later that month he moved his Chicago offices from the Metropole Hotel to the even grander Lexington and had it equipped with a vast menu of safety measures. Capone also made sure that, unlike Yale, his cars were fully protected, and he had his Cadillac fitted with bullet-proof glass, run-flat tires and a police siren. On December 8, 1941, President Franklin Delano Roosevelt rode to the Capitol to deliver his famous "Infamy" speech the day after Pearl Harbor in a heavily armored 1928 Cadillac 341A Town Sedan. That Cadillac had originally belonged to Al Capone, and it had been impounded after it was confiscated by Treasury Department officials during the investigation of Capone's finances.

As the fall election approached in 1928, Frank Loesch, the head of the Chicago Crime Commission, approached Capone and privately sought his intervention. Capone made sure the police, many of whom were on his payroll, were out in full force, and the election was a peaceful one.

The St. Valentine's Day Massacre

At the start of 1929, Capone's position appeared secure. A raid spearheaded by the new U.S. attorney George Johnson on his Chicago Heights operations seemed to be only a minor inconvenience at the time — little did Al know that ledgers seized during the raid would prove crucial in the government's tax evasion case. His brother Ralph was not nearly as clever as Al in covering up his financial tracks and would end up being a weak link.

Meanwhile, the never-ending feud with the North Side gangs continued to be a thorn in Capone's side. Bugs Moran, still bitter at Al for the Hymie Weiss hit, had tried repeatedly and unsuccessfully to assassinate him. Having failed so frequently in his attempted hits on Capone, Bugs now decided to go after one of Capone's right-hand men, "Machine Gun" Jack McGurn, a tough-nosed bodyguard who had risen to become a prominent partner in Capone's organization. McGurn was peppered with machine gun spray but somehow survived. After he recovered, he approached Capone with an ambitious plan to take out the entire Moran gang once and for all.

Machine Gun Jack McGurn

The scheme took weeks to put together, and involved dangling a cheap new supply of quality whiskey, with the intention of luring Bugs Moran to the SMC Cartage warehouse on North Clark Street. Moran took the bait, and on the morning of February 14, 1929, a bunch of Moran's crew turned up at the warehouse to wait for the shipment. At about 10:30, a car full of what appeared to be policemen pulled up to the garage where the drop was to take place. Thinking it was one of many sham raids in which the cops simply went through the motions and were really just after a bigger bribe, Moran's men let their guard down, dropped their guns and put their hands up. The "policemen" were in fact McGurn and his hand-picked crew, which mostly consisted of out-of-towners that Capone figured none of the North Side men would recognize.

Fortunately for Bugs Moran, he was running late to the warehouse, and as he and Ted Newberry headed toward the rear of the warehouse, they saw the police car pull up. Naturally, Moran and Newberry turned around and fled, at which point they ran into Henry Gusenberg and warned him to stay away. Another Moran associate, Willie Marks, spotted the police car and hid, making sure to take down the car's license plate number before fleeing.

With two of the "officers" having lined up the 7 men present against the rear wall of the garage, it seems that one of Moran's men, Albert Weinshank, was mistaken for Moran himself, a result of the fact that they were similar in size and stature and dressed similarly. Witnesses later explained that they saw four men, two dressed as cops, walk into the warehouse. Likely believing Weinshank was Bugs Moran, the two "cops" gave the signal to the pair in civilian clothes, and those two opened fire with tommy guns, ruthlessly slaughtering the defenseless men. For good measure, the bodies were also shot with shotguns, which all but blew off the faces of John May and James Clark. And to keep the ruse going, the four men emerged from the warehouse with the two "cops" escorting the two "civilians" with their hands up.

The St. Valentine's Day Massacre

As Capone's men fled the scene, one of the survivors began piping up: Highball, John May's German Shepherd. With the dog barking, bystanders and eventually authorities discovered the grisly scene, and somehow Frank Gusenberg was still alive. In fact, despite suffering 14 bullet wounds, he was still conscious. A famous legend is that as Gusenberg lay dying from the gunshot wounds, he told police that nobody shot him. Though this statement is probably apocryphal, nobody opened their mouths, and nobody was ever convicted for the "Saint Valentine's Day Massacre," the most famous gangland hit in American history, although Capone's involvement is unquestioned. It is widely believed that the 4 gunmen were Jack McGurn, John Scalise, Albert Anselmi, and Frank Rio, the bodyguard who had saved Capone from Moran's assassination attempt in 1926.

Scalise

It was a spectacular and notorious hit, but in many ways it backfired on Capone. The crew thought they had got Moran, but Bugs was in fact late for the meeting and had narrowly escaped. Though no one was ever charged or arrested, ballistics evidence linked McGurn to the crime and inevitably fingers started pointing toward Al. It was a black mark for the city of Chicago, and the national press produced a stream of sensational articles profiling Capone and his reign of terror in Chicago. The story even caught the eye of President Hoover, who began putting pressure on federal authorities to take action.

Capone Hides Out In Jail

For awhile, Al delighted in this new wave of notoriety, but he made a series of miscues that helped hasten his downfall. The growing pressure to do something about Capone led the Chicago U.S. Attorney George Johnson to issue a subpoena ordering him to appear before a federal grand jury on March 12. Capone delayed and feigned sickness. Though he ultimately showed up a week later, investigators were able to prove he was not in fact ill, opening him up to a contempt of court charge. But all the while Al carried himself with his characteristic bravado, assuming he would again find a way to escape charges.

Released at the moment from further questioning, it has been widely speculated that Capone returned to Chicago to discover that two of the gunmen who had been part of the St. Valentine's Day Massacre, Scalise and Anselmi, were seeking to turn on him and align themselves with fellow Sicilian Joseph Guinta, who had secretly formed an anti-Capone alliance with Joe Aiello (who Al had sent packing several years earlier). Capone threw an elaborate banquet for Guinta and the two gunmen—and after hours of food and drink turned on the three men with a baseball bat (a scene immortalized in the movie *The Untouchables*). It is believed that while Capone nearly beat them to death, he handed off the task of murdering them to his associates. The following day, the completely disfigured bodies of Scalise, Anselmi, and Joseph Giunta were discovered on a road near Hammond, Indiana. It was at first assumed that the North Side Gang had killed them in retaliation for the St. Valentine's Day Massacre, at least until it was discovered that the three men had been lured to a banquet with their Sicilian friends, making it far more likely that it was an inside job by Capone.

By now, even within the national community of racketeers and organized crime, Capone, with his increasingly volatile behavior and the attention he was drawing from federal authorities, was seen as a liability. That May, at a gathering in Atlantic City, a national Commission of racketeers presented him with a proposal that essentially involved the gradual dismantling of his empire for the good of all. The Commission was headed by none other than Al's old mentor, Johnny Torrio, unexpectedly emerged from retirement.

With the organized crime world now against him, and a target on his back from the federal government, Bugs Moran and countless other enemies, Capone seems to have panicked. He concocted a bizarre (but for the moment effective) scheme to have himself arrested in Philadelphia on a concealed weapons charge. And on May 18, 1929, Capone began a projected year-long sentence in a local county jail. He had, for now at least, avoided the day of reckoning.

Al Capone's cell at the Eastern State Penitentiary in Philadelphia

A New Decade, and a New World

Al's scheme threw law enforcement officials a bit of a curveball, but they continued to build their case against him, targeting brother Ralph as the weak link in the Capone organization. In what was seen as a test case in the new strategy, Ralph was arrested for tax evasion in early October. He was released on bail, with the trial set for May. But Ralph was sloppy and continued to provide the government with evidence gathered through law enforcement's latest technique of wire-tapping. Eliot Ness monitored Ralph's every move and conversation, and led a series of dramatic raids on the Capones' operations.

When Al Capone was finally released from a Pennsylvania prison on March 17, 1930 (two months early for good behavior), the world had changed. In October of the previous year, the stock market had crashed, sending the economy into a tailspin. In less than six months the number of unemployed had nearly doubled. The Roaring Twenties were over, and the nation was in a somber and sober mood. Though Capone's release landed him on the cover of *Time* magazine, he was no longer the folk hero he had once been. Frank Loesch of the Chicago Crime Commission, who Al had never taken seriously, developed an ingenius new media strategy by issuing a Public Enemies list, with Capone of course at Number 1. The idea was later adapted by

J. Edgar Hoover for the FBI's Most Wanted list. The tide had turned. The Commission had formed in 1919 among civic leaders aiming to work with the public to stop organized crime in the city. In addition to lobbying, the Commission put together records detailing organized crime in Chicago that were even better than the police had.

The Walls Close In

In April, Ralph stood trial for tax evasion and was quickly convicted. The government began pursuing other Capone associates, including Al's old friend Jack Guzik. Emboldened by the shift in public opinion and the new Public Enemy campaign, officials in Miami took aim at Al, threatening to arrest him on vague vagrancy charges or have his Palm Island villa declared a public nuisance. Public officials elsewhere followed suit, and though nothing came of it, Capone could not escape the nagging fear that the government was out to get him.

As the tax evasion cases against many of his friends went forward, Al tried his best to hold on. In November he opened up his own soup kitchen, feeding over 5,000 on Thanksgiving alone. In December his baby sister Mafalda was married and Al threw her a grand party. Though his brother and associates were going to jail, it was clear the government was having a tough time assembling a case against him. 1930 came to a close and he was still a free and powerful and rich man.

However, all throughout this time Frank Wilson, the Treasury investigator targeting Capone, was making slow but sure progress, succeeding in placing a double agent in Capone's organization and in "turning" a couple of former associates. Eliot Ness received all the headlines in the spring of 1931, but it was the June 5 indictment charging Al with 22 counts of tax evasion that was to be the backbreaker. Even then, Capone still had some tricks up his sleeve. He first attempted to make a plea deal, but after the judge warned he might not follow prosecutors' sentencing recommendations as part of that deal, Capone withdrew the guilty plea. He then plotted to bribe and intimidate potential jurors, but this was discovered by Ness and The Untouchables, who had the jury pool switched. Capone's luck had run out.

At the October trial Capone was convicted of only five counts, but that was enough to warrant an 11 year sentence. By the end of the month, Public Enemy Number 1 was in a Cook County Jail.

Capone in Prison

For a while, Al held out hope he would once more be able to wiggle out of his troubles. His brother Ralph had been sentenced to three years in federal prison, but was still at large while his lawyers filed appeals (though those appeals finally ran out in November). Meanwhile, the still formidable Capone set up shop at the county jail, made sure he had access to good food and even liquor, and continued to conduct business as usual. In the spring of 1932, with his legal team still filing appeals, Capone engaged in a last-ditch publicity stunt, offering to help find the kidnapped and missing son of Charles Lindbergh if he was released. But in May, Al's final appeal was denied, and he was shipped off to the Atlanta Penitentiary.

In Atlanta, Capone's health went into a long and steady decline, even as he engaged in ongoing legal maneuvers to attain an early release. Resentment over his special treatment in the Cook County Jail led to similar charges in Atlanta, not to mention the fact that he was widely suspected of continuing to carry out the Outfit's criminal enterprises from jail. Thus, in August of 1934 Capone was transferred to the recently opened federal facility of Alcatraz. His neurosyphilis began taking a toll on his mental as well as physical state, and, stripped of his old status and prestige, Al became a target of other prisoners and in 1936 was the object of a brutal stabbing attack. Two years later he suffered a serious mental breakdown and spent months in the prison hospital.

"The Rock", Alcatraz Island

Capone's cell in Alcatraz

When he was finally released in November of 1939, Capone was a broken man. His family sought experimental treatment for his syphilis at Johns Hopkins, which at best bought him some time. After four months he was released and traveled to his Palm Island Villa to live out his remaining years. He received visits from family and old associates, all monitored closely by the FBI. The visitors made small talk with Al, but he was not his old lucid self and was at times delusional, rambling at length about Communists and old foe Bugs Moran. Mental evaluations concluded that Capone had devolved into the mental ability of a 12 year old.

In 1945 he was one of the first civilians to be treated for syphilis with penicillin, but his health slowly but surely gave out, and on January 25 1947, just a week after his 48th birthday, Al "Scarface" Capone passed away after a stroke and cardiac arrest.

Chapter 7: The Man and the Myth

Despite his fame and high profile, Al Capone was hardly a model citizen, and there's no case to be made that he was on any level a good man. He was directly and indirectly responsible for the deaths of dozens of men. Perhaps, given the distorting effects of late-stage syphilis on his personality, it's impossible to know for certain who the "real" Capone was, but he was nonetheless a complicated man with surprising and unexpected dimensions.

A number of reporters and law enforcement officials, even those who disapproved of him and his lifestyle, found him charming and gracious. Those who spent time with him during his Lansing retreat, in particular, remember him as quite the opposite of the ruthless gangster portrayed in the media. In a period of American history characterized by narrow ethnic loyalty, Capone displayed a remarkable openness. He married an Irish girl. Among his associates and close friends were not only fellow Italians, but Irish and Jews. Finally, in addition to a love of opera (to be expected of someone of Italian heritage), Capone had a real love for the true music of the age: jazz. Not only did he love the music, he expressed a genuine affection for the men who played it—black musicians, at a time when the best blacks could expect was a kind of benign hostility. In contrast to his brother Ralph, for example (the actual manager of the Capone-run Cotton Club in Cicero), Al made a point of reaching out to and sometimes assisting the musicians who passed through.

With his dramatic life and outsized personality, it was perhaps inevitable that Capone the man would be swallowed up by Capone the myth. But two developments of the 1930s even further hastened the mythologizing of Al Capone. The first was a string of movies and books playing on (and often glamorizing) gangsters in the Capone mold. Notable among these were *Little Caesar*, starring Edwin G. Robinson, and the Howard Hawks-directed *Scarface* (later remade into a story about a Cuban gangster starring Al Pacino). It is also no accident that the comic strip *Dick Tracy* (often featuring larger-than-life gangsters bearing Tommy guns) debuted around this time. And, in real life, the Depression-era 30s ushered in a new breed of outlaw: including "Baby Face" Nelson, "Pretty Boy" Floyd, Bonnie and Clyde—and, most famously, John Dillinger, who topped the FBI's Most Wanted list just as Capone had topped the earlier Public Enemies list. Whereas Capone was the ultimate insider, and fundamentally a capitalist and businessman, the new breed consisted of outsiders and renegades, reflecting the alienation and disaffection of the era. Yet somehow in the public imagination, and in their many representations since in movies especially, the outlaws of the 20s and 30s have become fused and muddled.

To this day, the image of Capone continues to be evoked in the popular culture. Behind the curtain, the man himself remains a mystery.

John Dillinger and Baby Face Nelson

Chapter 1: Johnnie Dillinger

As with most of the other famous criminals of the era, it is not always easy to separate myth from reality in telling the story of John Dillinger. A major part of the narrative of Depression-era "outlaws" is that, in contrast to the "gangsters" of the 20s like Al Capone, they were country boys from America's heartland. For that very reason, some early versions of Dillinger's story portray him as a country boy from Mooresville, Indiana, even though his formative years were spent in the city and in prison.

It was Dillinger's father, John W. Dillinger, who was an authentic country boy, spending all of his first 23 years on various Indiana farms. In 1887 he married his wife, Mollie, a farmer's daughter from a nearby town. But sometime in the next two or three years, John Sr., along with his wife and baby girl Audrey, was forced to move to the city of Indianapolis to support his young family. For the next decade he worked various jobs as a manual laborer, gradually saving a bit of money, and in 1900 he invested his savings in a small grocery in the Oak Hill neighborhood of the city. He would run the store for the next 20 years, never moving outside a radius of a few blocks.

John Jr., known to most friends and family as Johnnie throughout his life, was born three years after his father opened the grocery store. By all accounts Johnnie had a perfectly normal childhood in respectable middle-class household. The only significant crisis of his childhood was the early loss of his mother, who fell ill shortly after giving birth to him and died three years later.

Some early chroniclers of Dillinger's life (most notably John Toland, whose *The Dillinger Days* was for many years the definite biography) purport to find in Dillinger's childhood early signs of his later criminal persona. They claim he had a chilly relationship with his stepmother and was involved in a youth gang called the Dirty Dozen. According to other accounts, Johnnie was a petty thief as a teen and was accused of being a bully with a "bewildering personality".

However, later biographers such as Elliott Gorn find the evidence for these stories spotty at best. Extensive interviews with family and neighbors paint a picture of an unremarkable boy who got into the occasional skirmish but was reasonable well behaved. By all outward appearances, nothing seemed to suggest the making of a future Public Enemy, though he did have the kind of charisma from an early age that would be on full display during his later criminal career. John Sr. described his son as having an unusual degree of "wit", "verve" and "self-reliance."[9]

As the nation geared up for World War I, work as a manual laborer was abundant and paid well. After eighth grade, Dillinger dropped out of school and worked various jobs, including as a machinist, for the next few years. Aside from an occasional extended leave of absence, the future outlaw seems to have been a reasonably good worker.

If the loss of his mother was the first significant disruption in Johnnie's young life, the family's move to the country in early 1920 was the second. Nearing 60 years of age, and with his children

---

[9] Gorn, *Dillinger's Wild Ride*, p. 7

entering their young adult years, John Sr. decided to return to his rural roots. He sold his grocery store and bought a small farm outside his second wife's hometown of Mooresville, where he and his new wife joined the local Quaker congregation and soon became every bit as respectable a family in the country as they'd been in the city.

Johnnie was 17 at the time, but he never quite adjusted to farm life. He suffered from hay fever and felt more at home in the nearby town of Martinsville, and he even traveled frequently back to Indianapolis to stay with his older sister Audrey. Dillinger did date a local farm girl, but the girl's father prevented the young couple from marrying. Dillinger apparently took this turn of events badly; and eventually he stole a car from a church parking lot and drove it to Indianapolis. The police found him, but in the first of many escapes Johnnie gave them the slip and ran to enroll in the Navy.[10]

Johnnie's first stint as a country boy had lasted less than half a year.

Chapter 2: Young Lester Gillis

Lester Joseph Gillis was born on December 6, 1908 in a back alley flat on California Avenue on the south side of Chicago. He was the seventh child of Josef and Mary Gillis, Belgians who had immigrated to Chicago from Nova Scotia but found not so much a land of opportunity as a dark, smelly neighborhood where the sun was never quite strong enough to completely drive away the shadow of local smokestacks. Josef worked more than 70 hours a week as a packer at the Union Stockyards, while Mary cared for Lester and his six older siblings and helping make ends meet by tutoring school children in French. Delicate and devout, she believed the best about most people, especially her children, but while she and Josef worked, their sons would roam the streets around the stockyard getting into petty mischief.

While Lester's older brothers soon outgrew their childhood shenanigans, Lester was different. For one thing, he regularly skipped school, until it reached the point that teachers expected him to be absent more than they expected him to be in class, and Lester dropped out entirely after the eighth grade. Perhaps part of the problem was his size. At 5'4," Lester was often the victim of bullies and miscreants who teased him about both his size and his innocent babyface. Of course, they also found it good fun to try to scar up that face with hits and cuts.

Before long, Lester had had all he could take. One day he came out swinging and learned that he felt better when he hit back. Over the next few months he gained a reputation for being more trouble than he was worth, and soon enough even the neighborhood "toughs" who were bigger than him would cross the street when they saw him coming.

Josef and Mary tried to intervened, first with a talking, then with yelling and eventually with a

---

[10] Gorn, *Dillinger's Wild Ride*, p. 9

razor strap. The local parish priest and the nuns who taught him at school also tried through encouragement and prayer to correct the tough little boy. However, it soon became apparent that there was something going on with Lester that went beyond the abilities of the local clergy or those of anyone else in the neighborhood either.

Soon Gillis was roaming the backstreets just looking for trouble. The Deering Street police knew that if a window was randomly smashed or a store front graffittied, it was likely the work of young Lester, as well as his friend Jack Perkins. The same theory applied to everything from stolen apples to pinched pocket knives. At first, they tried to scold the boys and talk to their parents, but it soon became apparent that that was not going to be enough to deter the growing delinquent. Perkins would later state that since Gillis was the smallest member of their group of petty thieves, he usually was the kid who got the attention at the store counter and diverted the notice of the clerk while the other boys committed the thefts. In hindsight, it might be that Gillis tried to overcompensate for his perceived physical shortcomings by acting tougher and acting out even more wildly.

Lester's worst early crime was an accident. On July 4, 1921, while watching some Independence Day festivities with friends, he pulled out a pistol he'd found around town, probably thrown away by an escaping felon. The boys gathered around to look at it and Gillis accidentally pulled the trigger, shooting one of his friends in the jaw. Though the boy recovered, he was permanently maimed and Gillis was sent to the state reformatory for a year.

In 1920, at the age of 12, Gillis stole his first car. He continued with auto theft until the following year, when he was caught, arrested and convicted, receiving a sentence of a year in the local juvenile hall. As soon as he got out, he stole another car, got caught again, and was sentenced to 18 month in jail. When the teenager was away this time, Josef committed suicide. Concerned that his life of crime had driven his father to take his life, Gillis began sending money home to his mother every chance he got.

Due to some violent incidents between him and the other boys, Gillis was not released from juvenile hall until almost two years later. By then he had learned all the tricks to the criminal trade and went immediately back to the streets, robbing and pillaging small time grocery stores and local department stores. It only took five months for him to be arrested again, this time for breaking into a department store. Caught in the act, Gillis was sent to the Chicago Boys Home, a dark, creepy building with more troubled boys than the small staff could begin to handle.

Chapter 3: Dillinger's First Stint in Jail

The Navy gave Dillinger shelter from the police after he concocted a story about being from St. Louis, but he didn't fit in there any better than he had on the farm. He made it successfully through basic training, but shortly after being transferred to a ship in Boston in October, he failed to return from shore leave and was declared AWOL. He returned on his own, only to be fined and put in solitary confinement for 10 days, but the punishment didn't correct his behavior. He got in trouble shortly thereafter and was again put in solitary. In December he left for good after being dishonorably discharged from the Navy. Dillinger returned to Mooresville, claiming the Navy had discharged him for a heart murmur.

Back at home, Dillinger fell in love with another local farm girl, Beryl Ethel Hovious, and in April 1924 the young couple was married. Though his wife characterized him as charming and well-mannered in later interviews, it became clear early on that the newly married Dillinger wasn't quite cut out for the quiet life. He began frequenting local pool halls, both in Mooresville and in the nearby town of Martinsville, where he seems to have first developed friendships with the kind of shady comrades who would shape the next phase of his life.

Chief amongst these was a man in his young thirties named Edward Singleton. The two men decided to engineer a modest stickup, choosing an elderly local grocer, Frank Morgan, as their target. It is impossible to ignore the coincidence that Dillinger's first victim was a man who very much resembled his own father. Moreover, Dillinger knew the man and frequently shopped in his store.

As it turned out, the first hold-up committed by America's most famous bank robber was an utter fiasco. During the stickup, Dillinger struck Morgan over the head with a pipe, and when the old man attempted to call for help, Dillinger pulled a gun on him. The gun went off accidentally, and Dillinger and his accomplice fled with $50.

Clearly new to this line of work, Dillinger mistakenly implicated himself by asking around town about the grocer's well-being even before the botched hold-up had been reported. Not surprisingly, the police soon tracked the young man down and arrested him. At the advice of his father, Dillinger made a full confession and threw himself at the mercy of the court, while Singleton, on the other hand, pled innocent and hired a lawyer. Dillinger's strategy backfired; the judge decided to make an example of him and sentenced him to 10-20 years at the Indiana State Reformatory at Pendleton.[11]

As a result, Dillinger spent most of his 20s in prison, and it was there that he became the man who would briefly but spectacularly terrorize the Midwest. 80 years later, biographers and historians still disagree as to exactly when and how Johnnie Dillinger transformed from a troubled young adult into the brazenly suave Public Enemy Number 1. Some have argued that Dillinger was bitter from the start about being unfairly singled out for harsh punishment and vowed to become an even more hardened criminal once he got out. Others have countered that the shift took place only later during his prison term.

What is clear is that Dillinger was constantly getting into trouble almost from the day he

---

[11] Gorn, *Dillinger's Wild Ride*, p. 13

entered prison on September 16, 1924. Most of his infractions were minor, but he also hid from the guards and attempted a few early escapes. He spent a good deal of time in solitary confinement for his troubles and had his sentence increased, but he managed to maintain high spirits, as evidenced in letters written to his family. Dillinger also apparently became acquainted with like-minded men, including Charles Makley, Russell Clark, and Homer Van Meter, all of whom eventually ran with his gang. It's believed that it was Homer Van Meter who taught Dillinger the science of crime, and it's been suggested that these men actually began planning their future robberies while still in jail.

Homer Van Meter

1929 was a pivotal year for Dillinger. That spring, his young wife, to whom he'd only been properly married for five months, finally filed for divorce. Soon after, the parole board turned down his appeal for an early release. Later that year he was transferred to the state prison in Michigan City. The new facility was tougher than the one in Pendleton, but it appears Dillinger lobbied for the move in order to be with some friends who'd recently been transferred there. At any rate, his troubles continued, with minor infractions and a second escape attempt frequently landing him in solitary. He seems to have hit bottom in 1932, writing to his younger brother Hubert: "It seems like I can't keep out of trouble here… I guess I am just incorrigible."[12]

However, at some point in 1932 another shift seems to have taken place. Dillinger managed to stay out of trouble and began actively planning for another appeal to the parole board the following year. Some historians make a convincing case that Harry Pierpont, a fellow convict who'd been trying for years to escape, targeted Dillinger (the most likely to be paroled first) as

---

[12] Gorn, *Dillinger's Wild Ride*, p. 19

his way out—convincing him of the wealth and adventure that could be theirs if they worked as a team to gain one another's freedom.[13] Indeed, in just a few short months, Dillinger would be instrumental in helping Pierpont break out of jail, only to have Pierpont return the favor shortly thereafter.

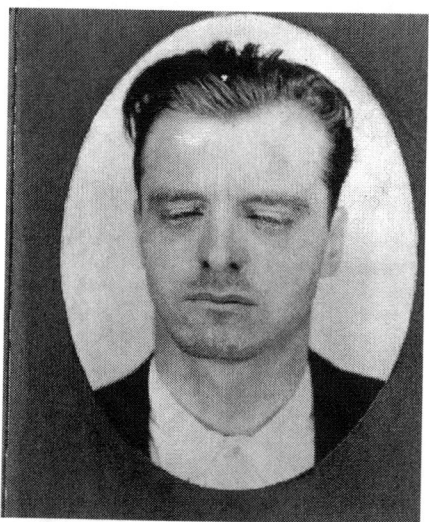

Pierpont's mugshot

Dillinger's second appearance before the parole board in early 1933 was more auspicious than his first. He had deliberately lined up the cards in his favor, getting his family to orchestrate a careful campaign that included a petition in Mooresville, and letters of support not only from his victim Frank Morgan but from the judge who had sentenced him in the first place. Other circumstances were also on Dillinger's side; with the Depression and the new crime wave wreaking havoc, prison overcrowding was becoming a serious problem.

The board ruled in Dillinger's favor, and in May he was back "home" in Mooresville. Just shy of 30 years old, Dillinger had spent nearly the entire decade of his 20s behind bar, and he returned to a vastly different world. FDR had been sworn into office just two months earlier, reminding the country that the only thing they had to fear "was fear itself", and soon after entering office the new president declared a four-day national "bank holiday" to prevent panic from spreading through the banking system. In the cities, workers were striking. In Dillinger's rural Midwest, farms fell victim to foreclosure, and the region was hit by a long-term drought that in the coming years would produce the devastation of the Dust Bowl. The nation, in short,

---

[13] Burroughs, *Public Enemies*, p. 139

was unsettled and uneasy.

Dillinger, in the eyes of some chroniclers, had already settled on a plan to pursue a life of crime, and in prison had forged alliances with the men who would help him do it. According to this version of events, Dillinger even went so far as to study bank-robbing, notably the innovative system devised by Herman Lamm, a German bank robber who cased his targets and used getaway drivers, lookouts, a lobby man, and a vault man. Dillinger would befriend two of the men who robbed banks with Lamm, Walter Dietrich and James "Oklahoma Jack" Clark, thereby learning about Lamm's system from men who had participated in it.

Lamm

On the other hand, some accounts at least raise the possibility that, for a time, Dillinger considered going "straight." He attended church, apologized to his victim Frank Morgan, and visited his ex-wife. Still, Dillinger had made a half-hearted attempt at being a family man 10 years earlier, but he wouldn't even really bother trying this time around. Dillinger had only 14 more months to live, and he would make every day count.

Chapter 4: Becoming Baby Face Nelson

When Gillis was released in the fall of 1926, the 18 year old thug found a whole new world of crime waiting for him. The Eighteenth Amendment to the Constitution, also known as the Volstead Act, made it illegal to produce, sell or consume alcoholic beverages. Unbeknownst to the politicians and zealous temperance advocates, the American public responded to being told that they couldn't drink by wanting to drink even more. Though Prohibition was ultimately a poorly conceived and poorly implemented disaster, it is not as simple a story as it might first appear to be. The Temperance Movement, as it was first known, dated all the way back to the 1840s, when drinking was an undeniable problem in American life. Historians estimate that per capita consumption of booze was as high as 7 gallons of pure alcohol a year, well over three times the current rate, and the equivalent of 90 bottles of 80-proof liquor a year. In response to this very real problem, groups like the Daughters of Temperance began cropping up, and later the Women's Christian Temperance Union. The Prohibition Party was founded in 1872, but it was the Anti-Saloon League, founded in 1893, that made prohibition a viable political force.

The reason Prohibition proved such a disaster was that there were plenty of underworld characters and organized crime networks fully intending to profit from it by smuggling and secretly brewing liquor. By 1926, as young Gillis was coming of age and getting into more trouble, the head of these illegal efforts to quench American thirst was reigning kingpin Al Capone, who had risen to the command of one of Chicago's most powerful mobs through brute force in the 1920s.

Scarface

According to one legend that some scholars now dispute, Gillis began working for Capone's Chicago Outfit after hearing that Capone was hiring "enforcers," thugs that would act as armed guards to keep away any cops that hadn't already been bribed into cooperation. They also knocked off the competition and protected products being moved from one location to another. Gillis jumped at a chance to get paid for bullying people, a skill he had already perfected while selling protection services to local small (and often criminal) businessmen.

As the story goes, perhaps embellished to make Gillis sound even more dangerous, Capone and his crew grew concerned with the violence Gillis used to collect overdue payments. After all, if a customer was dead, or even just seriously injured, he couldn't work enough to pay what he owed. Also, many of the underworld people he was dealing with were themselves members of the Sicilian Mafia, and Capone couldn't risk making them too mad. While they understood the need for enforcement, they were never fans of violence just for violence's sake. For those reasons, Capone's method was always to threaten rather than act when possible, but Gillis, on the other hand, preferred to hit first and talk later.

At first, Jack McGurn, Capone's lieutenant in charge of the enforcers and the man believed responsible for plotting the notorious St. Valentine's Day Massacre in 1929, tried to reason with Gillis. He explained several times that it was better to leave men afraid than maimed. Gillis, however, simply could not control himself, especially when he tasted blood. When he fought, he would often stop only when his victim was nearly dead. Unable to control him, McGurn finally had to let him go. Though furious, Gillis still had enough self-control not to cross the most powerful gangster in Chicago.

"Machine Gun" Jack McCurn

In 1928, Gillis met the only woman that he would ever love. Helen Wawzynak was working as a salesgirl in a Chicago Woolworth's when they started dating. He called her his "Million Dollar Baby From the Five and Ten Cent Store", and she was captivated by Gillis's boyish good looks and sideways smile. When they had only been dating a few months, he began to suggest they get married. However, her family was against it, and she was unable to marry without their permission because she was still just 16. Things changed a few months later when she turned up pregnant. Gillis robbed a jewelry store just outside Wheaton, put a hot ring on her finger, and used the rest of the loot to set them up in a little house in the suburbs. Their son Ronald was born in April 1930, six months after they married, and a daughter named Darlene would follow in 1932.

By the time he met his future wife, Gillis had the only respectable job he would ever hold, working for a Standard Oil Station near his home. But even then, he had a few underhanded dealings going on. He began by looking the other way while a gang of tire thieves used his station for their headquarters. Through them he met some bootleggers who hired him to haul their wares out of town to the Chicago suburbs.

One of the men Gillis worked for was Roger Touhy, a rival of Capone's and head of the infamous Touhy Gang, a mob that bootlegged liquor in the northwest suburbs of Chicago. Working with them, he quickly graduated from petty crime to armed robbery. In January 1930, the gang broke into the home of magazine executive Charles M. Richter and took more than $25,000 in jewelry. Prior to leaving, they bound him with adhesive tape and cut off his phone lines so their victim could not alert the police. After a similar robbery in March of the home of banker Lottie Brenner Von Beulow, in which they made off with $50,000 in jewels, Gillis and the others had been dubbed "The Tape Bandits".

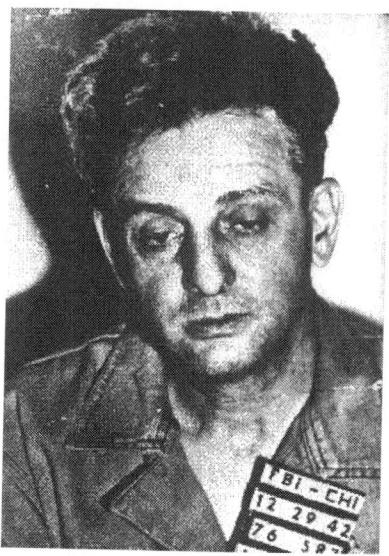

Roger Touhy

Gillis was just getting warmed up. A few months later, on April 21, 1930, he pulled his first bank job, making off with $4,000 in cash. In early October, Gillis and his cronies robbed the Itasca State Bank, making off with $4,600, and three days later, they brazenly broke into the home of Mayor Bill Thompson of Chicago and stole more than $18,000 worth of his wife's jewelry. When she described Gillis to the police, she said, "He had a baby face. He was good looking, hardly more than a boy, had dark hair and was wearing a gray topcoat and a brown felt hat, turned down brim."

Mayor "Big Bill" Thompson

No doubt flushed with their success, the Tape Bandits were back at it the following month. That November, they attempted to rob a restaurant in Summit, Illinois. This time, however, the attempt went completely haywire. It turned out that several of the patrons were themselves armed and fired on the would-be robbers, touching off a gunfight that left three bystanders dead and three others wounded. While it's unclear whether Gillis had fired any of the fatal shots in that encounter, he definitely committed murder days later on November 26, 1930, shooting and killing wealthy stockbroker Edwin R. Thompson while they robbed his home.

Despite their successful and notorious crime spree, the Tape Bandits were finally arrested in early 1931, including Gillis, who used the alias George Nelson. The press would later couple this alias with Mrs. Thompson's description, dubbing him "Baby Face Nelson" and referring to him as the leader of the group.

After he was convicted, Nelson was sentenced to a prison sentence of one to ten years in Joliet, the infamous Illinois State Penitentiary, but after he had already been imprisoned, he was charged and convicted of another crime he had previously committed, a bank robbery in Wheaton, Illinois. This added charge brought his sentence up to possible life in prison.

Nelson, of course, had other plans. When he learned that he would be transported from his trial in Wheaton back to Joliet by train and then police car on February 17, 1932, he arranged for Helen to hide a gun for him in the train station men's room. While he may have been a little nervous about trying to take on several officers in a fully outfitted police car, he soon found out luck was on his side. Upon departing from the train, the officer in charge learned that there was no police car yet dispatched to pick them up. Rather than wait for another official vehicle, the officer simply hailed a cab and loaded his prisoner into the back seat.

All was well for a few minutes until they were well clear of the station. Then Nelson whipped out the hand gun, shoved it in the surprised cop's face and growled, "Don't give me a reason to kill you." He then ordered the driver to pull over and forced both men out of the car. With his gun still pointed at the officer's head, Nelson moved to the driver's seat and drove off, leaving the cab driver and the policeman beside the road with no way to call help.

Free once again, Nelson initially traded on his connections with the Touhy Gang to make his way to Reno, Nevada, where he hid out in the underworld then growing up around Las Vegas and went by the names Jimmy Burnett and Jimmy Burnell. He met William Graham, one of the gambling crime bosses that populated that part of the country. The two focused mostly on stealing cars, which drew the attention of law enforcement officers on the look-out for the escaped prisoner. According to those questioned, the suspect had a wife he called his "million dollar baby," as well as an infant son.

Next, he moved on to Sausalito, California, where he met John Paul Chase. Like Nelson, Chase had a reputation as a small time hood and bootlegger. The two men hit it off and were soon close friends. Chase introduced Nelson to Sicilian mobster Joe Parente, who was always looking to add another crooked limb to his criminal family tree. Before long, Nelson was doing everything from acting as a bodyguard to cracking safes and driving truckloads of liquor around the state.

Parente kept several small bungalows around Sausalito as hideouts, which allowed Nelson to move into one with Helen and baby Ronald. While they were living there, Helen gave birth to Darlene. When not robbing banks or running moonshine, he seemingly lived the life of a quiet suburban father, mowing the grass, taking the family picnicking, swimming in the ocean and sitting on the porch with his family.

While in California, Nelson made much of his living selling Parente's product to sometimes reluctant buyers. He would swagger into a speakeasy and asked to see the manager. When he came out, Nelson would inform him that he would now be serving only product supplied by Parente. If the manager took exception to this proposition, Nelson would elaborate on the sad "accidents" that had befallen others who rejected the offer. The manager would usually get the message and Nelson would usually get the credit.

However, Nelson was hardly the only tough in Sausalito playing this game. At times, when he tried to move in on another boss's territory, Nelson would find that it was his life in danger, not that of his potential customer. When this happened, he would usually contact some of Parente's other men and a battle, either literal or figurative, would ensue.

When not working for Parente, Chase and Nelson dreamed of being their own men and robbing their way into wealth and prosperity, and they shared these aspirations with their new friends, Tommy Carroll and Eddie Green. While Green and Carroll were also working for Parente at that time, they still had wonderful tales to tell of their own crime spree days, when they worked their way across the Midwest robbing small town banks as they passed through and then speeding out of town before the authorities could catch them. For a criminally ambitious man like Nelson, the small towns to the Midwest sounded like the perfect land of opportunity.

One name also stood out in many of their stories: John Dillinger. If the Midwest was the Promised Land, then Dillinger was the evil messiah for all penny ante crooks. Carroll and Green both claimed to have pulled jobs for Dillinger, and Nelson began to long to meet this legendary crime figure who had already robbed more banks than any other "public enemy" of that time.

Chapter 5: Dillinger Becomes Famous

"I'm not guilty of everything they have on me." – John Dillinger

One of the reasons it's unclear whether Dillinger tried to go straight or go straight to crime is that he may or may not have been involved in a crime spree conducted just a month after his release. According to many of the first histories of Dillinger's life, the future celebrity outlaw wasted no time in beginning his historic crime spree by robbing a bank in Ohio of $10,000. A week later, three men attempted to steal the payroll of a local thread mill in Indiana. This was followed by a series of stickups and yet another bank robbery.

Some have attributed all of these heists to Dillinger and his friends from prison, but the only evidence to back this claim is the testimony of one of Dillinger's early accomplices, William Shaw. Shaw's brief connection to Dillinger was his only link to fame, and over the years his story grew and expanded. Matt Leach, the chief of the Indiana state police, was the man who interrogated Shaw, and his accounts too show clear signs of exaggeration. Just a few months later, for example, Leach would declare to the press that Dillinger's gang had been responsible for 24 bank robberies in sixty days—a figure he seems to have pulled from thin air.[14] Given that Dillinger would be the most famous outlaw in America by the end of 1933 and his legend would only continue to grow in 1934, it's no surprise that accounts of his activity became more exaggerated over time. J. Edgar Hoover turned the Dillinger case into the crowning feather in the FBI's cap, and everyone who had ever brushed elbows with the famous outlaw wanted to tell his story. Naturally, the more dramatic the details, the better the story.

But did Dillinger actually participate in these crimes? It seems far more likely that Dillinger, as his father claimed, spent those first few months looking for work, hanging around the farm, and spending time with the family. He even reportedly had a particular fondness for one of his nieces. Unfortunately, these were not good times for a newly released convict to try to go straight, with the Depression in full swing and the farm life being even harder to maintain in the Midwest. Dillinger had just spent over 9 years with ambitious criminals, and the world Dillinger knew best was the criminal network he had come to know in prison. This was his comfort zone, and in the end, that was what he fell back on.

What everyone can agree on is that Dillinger was conducting heists by the summer of 1933. On July 17, less than two months after Dillinger's release, two men robbed a bank in Daleville, Indiana, and this robbery bears many of the telltale signs of Dillinger's future heists. The men were calm and collected, and one of them nimbly leapt over the bank counter. A bank teller later identified Dillinger from a photo and described the signature scar on his upper lip.

In early August, Dillinger, his prison pal Harry Copeland, and another man hit a bank in Indiana, and a week later they hit another one in Ohio. They may have done some smaller jobs that month as well, but their biggest score came on September 3rd when they walked away with $25,000 from a bank in Indianapolis. What is striking about this initial string of robberies was the group's efficiency and organization. The robberies themselves were conducted calmly and coolly, and it was clear that the hits had been well researched and that all the necessary preparations were in place. The robbers made their getaways in stolen vehicles with recycled license plates. They were well armed, and knew whom to contact to sell items like stolen bonds. It's believed that the gang at this point consisted of Shaw and Copeland, as well as Homer Van Meter, who had been paroled four days before Dillinger from the same prison.[15]

The gang also knew where to lay low while they were between jobs. Going back to Prohibition and even before then, brothels had become an important meeting ground among the criminal underground, and it seems Dillinger made up for time lost in prison. He also picked up a regular girlfriend, Mary Longnaker, who he wrote letters to while he was out on the road.

---

[14] Gorn, *Dillinger's Wild Ride*, p. 42
[15] Gorn, *Dillinger's Wild Ride*, p. 32

Though not yet known to the general public or the press, Dillinger began appearing on the radar of various law enforcement officials and investigators in Indiana, and his parole officer began staking out the Dillinger home in Mooresville after becoming suspicious. One of the banks he had hit hired an insurance investigator who would be on Dillinger's trail for months and turn up some important leads. On top of that, Matt Leach of the Indiana State Police, his tendency to exaggerate notwithstanding, began working his contacts in the criminal world and in prison. Dillinger would quickly have all the heat he could handle.

It was the Fall of 1933 when Dillinger's budding career as an outlaw would go big-time. He had developed an extensive network of future accomplices while in prison, and not only had they been scheming together but likely were discussing which targets to hit. It's presumed that the robbers were also able to communicate with those who were still locked up. Dillinger liked these men, felt loyal to them, and shared with them a resentment toward the "system" that they felt had wronged them.

Chief among these comrades was Harry Pierpont, credited by many with being the true leader of the gang in the early days. In mid-September, Dillinger made an unsuccessful attempt to smuggle guns into the Michigan City prison where Pierpont and others were still housed. Soon after, he made another attempt, successfully packaging them in large thread spools used in the prison's work camp.

By the end of the month, Pierpont and nine others would be free men, but not before Dillinger had been captured. Acting on a tip from the insurance investigator, Dayton police had staked out Mary Longnaker's apartment. Three days after Dillinger smuggled the guns into the Michigan City prison, he himself was once more in prison. While authorities decided where Dillinger would stand trial, he remained at a relatively unfortified jail in Lima, Ohio. Early newspaper accounts of his arrest didn't even mention his name, instead referring to him by the nickname "Jackrabbit", based on his trademark leap over bank counters.

Ironically, Dillinger would become famous just as he was imprisoned. The jailbreak at Michigan City suddenly raised Dillinger's profile as newspaper accounts referred to the men as "Dillinger's Gang." It is likely that his style and charm simply made for better newspaper copy, even though at this point it appears Harry Pierpont was the clear leader of the gang. At any rate, Pierpont and the other recent escaped convicts weren't about to let Dillinger's favor go unrewarded. On the night of October 12, six men broke their friend out of the Lima jail, fatally wounding Sheriff Jess Sarber in the process while impersonating Indiana State Officers who were supposedly there to extradite Dillinger. The second local jailbreak in two weeks was big news, even warranting a mention in the *New York Times*. Dillinger had become a national figure.[16]

As if these jailbreaks weren't spectacular enough, the newly expanded gang wasted no time in moving on to an equally audacious strategy: conducting raids of local police stations to stock up on arms. Two nights after Dillinger's rescue, the group hit a station in Auburn, Indiana. A week later they hit another Indiana station and made off with a variety of weapons, including Thompson machine guns, and bulletproof vests.

Newly fortified, the gang hit a bank in Greencastle, Indiana on October 23, making away with another $25,000. In the following two days, three more local banks were hit, but those involved smaller scores and may not have been the work of the Dillinger and Pierpont gang. But that didn't stop the press, now officially in high alert mode, from jumping to conclusions. Over-the-top stories on the gang were a daily occurrence, referring to them as "desperadoes" and even "terrorists." Law enforcement officials followed suit, with the Indian governor mobilizing the National Guard and deputizing 70 new officers and 500 soldiers.

The heat was on, and Dillinger and the gang wisely laid low for a while. Using their underworld contacts, they acquired apartments for themselves and their girlfriends, largely in the North Side of Chicago. For much of November they largely stayed out of sight, spending their money and enjoying themselves.

By now, the "Dillinger gang" was so notorious that other bank robbers and underworld members wanted to be part of the gang. One young hood who was from the Midwest and wanted in was Baby Face Nelson. In 1933, things in California were getting too hot for Baby Face to continue to work there, so that May, he and the rest of his family headed to Long Beach, Indiana, where he soon hooked up with several other bank robbers, including Edward Bentz, Tommy Carroll, Earl Doyle and Homer Van Meter. Nelson hoped that Van Meter would prove to be his connection to Dillinger.

---

[16] Gorn, *Dillinger's Wild Ride,* pp. 35-42

The two men met in an Indiana bar one evening to drink and talk things over, but right from the start Nelson rubbed Van Meter the wrong way. The veteran of Michigan State Prison found the short little man with the funny nickname a joke and even told him so. Enraged, Nelson considered answering back but quickly thought better of it. Even he had more common sense than to tick off Dillinger's Number 2 man. The more Nelson tried to quote his experience and recommendations, the more Van Meter blew him off. In the end, Nelson decided that if he couldn't make it into Dillinger's famous inner circle, he'd create one for himself.

The first step toward this goal was to really learn the art of bank robbing. To do this, Nelson began putting the word out at the infamous Green Lantern Tavern in St. Paul. There he ran into Carroll and Green again, who had recently blown into town from California. No big fans of Dillinger themselves, they were glad to have Nelson and Chase team up with them, and together the four started robbing small banks across the Midwest, usually focusing their attentions on Iowa, Nebraska and Wisconsin.

Their method was always the same: burst in the doors, shoot off a couple of machine guns in the air to get everyone's attention, grab the guards and take their weapons, push all the customers and most of the employees into a corner where they could be easily watched, force another employee to open the safe, grab as much money as they quickly could, fire over everyone's heads one more time and make for the getaway car. Typically, Nelson was the first in and the last out, cursing and yelling at everyone to remove their valuables and drop them in a bag he passed around. His most notorious bank robbery during the period was an August 1933 bank robbery in Grand Haven, Michigan, which went haywire but ultimately resulted in the robbers getting away clean. As Baby Face Nelson and his gang became more sophisticated, Homer Van Meter would form a second opinion in early 1934 about letting him run with the Dillinger gang.

When things heated up in Minnesota in October of 1933, Nelson decided to take his family and his newly organized gang south to hide out. They landed in San Antonio, Texas, where the men made contact with Hyman Lebman, a well-known gunsmith who was only too happy to hook them up with new weapons to use in their future robberies. Among these was a .38 Colt fully automatic pistol that would become one of Nelson's favorite weapons.

Ironically, San Antonio soon proved to be hotter than Minnesota. On December 9, one of his neighbors called the police about a bunch of "high powered Northern gangsters". A couple of days later, two detectives, H. C. Perrin and Al Hartman moved in on Tommy Carroll, who decided to go down fighting. He killed Perrin and wounded Harman before escaping back to warn the gang. Everyone scattered, with Nelson taking his family to San Francisco, where he began a new string of robberies the following spring.

At the same time, despite the Dillinger gang's underworld contacts and their best efforts to keep a low profile, law enforcement officials were closing in. Police had their own criminal contacts, and they had developed a list of suspicious apartments that were targeted in unsuccessful raids. But the insurance investigator had managed to create a snitch by "turning" Arthur McGinnis, who had served time with Dillinger, into a paid informant. McGinnis offered to sell some of the bank bonds Dillinger and Pierpont had stolen, and in the process learned Dillinger was experiencing a skin problem and would be seeing a local dermatologist on November 15. Matt Leach mobilized a team to take down Dillinger after the doctor's appointment, but Dillinger's new girlfriend, "Billie" Frechette, seems to have tipped him off, and the two escaped.

Billie Frechette

Dillinger and the gang could have played it safe, but they decided to go for one last big score before the Holidays. They hit a bank in Racine, Wisconsin on November 20, 1933, and though they walked away with a good deal of cash, this was not exactly the smooth operation of previous heists. The head teller and at least two policemen were shot (though not fatally), and several hostages were taken as shields before being released once the gang had escaped.

The gang got away successfully, but the police were making headway. Dillinger's early accomplice Harry Copeland, not involved in the Racine heist, was arrested three days earlier. And in mid-December, John "Red" Hamilton was identified in Chicago and approached by Sergeant William Shanley. As Shanley attempted to search Hamilton, he shot the officer fatally. Shanley's murder on the streets of Chicago had suddenly raised the stakes. The city assembled its own "Dillinger Squad," and Melvin Purvis, head of the local branch of the Bureau of

Investigation (soon to be renamed the FBI) wrote his boss about the matter. Dillinger was now on J. Edgar Hoover's radar as well. Though bank robbery was still not a federal crime, the gang had transported a stolen car across state lines when they'd broken Dillinger out, and that was a federal crime.

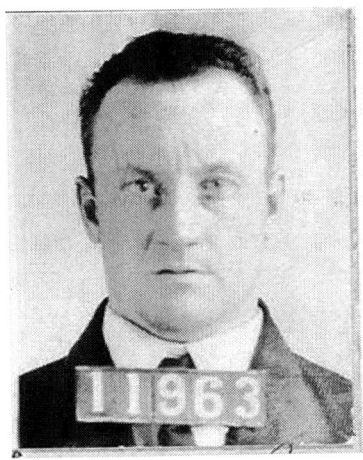

Red Hamilton

In December most of the gang headed to Florida, arriving on the 19th at Daytona Beach, where they rented a beach house and successfully kept a low profile for the rest of the year. Back in Chicago, the Illinois attorney general declared Dillinger "Public Enemy Number One." Moreover, the rest of the top ten were all members of the gang or associates of Dillinger. Dillinger's first documented heist had been in July; in less than five months, he had emerged from obscurity to become America's most notorious outlaw. And his adventures were just beginning.

Purvis

Chapter 6: Dillinger and Baby Face Join Forces

At the start of 1934, the Dillinger gang had decided for various reasons to convene in Tucson, Arizona, a place they felt they could go undetected. But in mid-January, while most of the gang was already in Tucson, Dillinger and his girlfriend Billie made a detour in East Chicago. Dillinger later claimed he was still in Florida, but while it is understandable why he wanted to distance himself from the events of January 15, evidence indicates otherwise.[17]

Just before closing time at the First National Bank of East Chicago, two men later identified as Dillinger and Hamilton entered the bank. Dillinger pulled out a submachine gun and calmly announced, as he always did, that this was a stickup. Someone triggered an alarm; but Dillinger had encountered that before and remained unfazed. By the time all the money was bagged, the bank was surrounded by police; but that, too, was not new to Dillinger. With a police officer and a bank vice-president in front of him as a human shield, Dillinger proceeded to the door.

But what was new this time was that one of the policemen outside, William O'Malley, thought he could take Dillinger down. He yelled for the officer Dillinger was holding to duck and opened fire. The outlaw fired back. Dillinger was hit, but he was wearing a bulletproof vest and was unharmed. However, O'Malley was fatally wounded, and Dillinger's partner was also seriously hurt. The two got away, but the game had changed for Dillinger; for the first time, he was directly implicated in the killing of a police officer.

---

[17] Burroughs, *Public Enemies*, p. 188

Hamilton was treated for his wounds but would have to lay low for some time as he slowly recovered. Dillinger reconnected with Billie and the two took an indirect route to Tucson, stopping along the way to briefly visit Dillinger's father, and then in St. Louis to change cars. Eventually they reconnected with the rest of the gang in Tucson.

It would take very little time for the Feds to catch up with them. Following a timely tip from a couple who had provided the gang some assistance, along with a few untimely instances of indiscretion by members of the gang, the local police, tipped off by the Feds, had the gang's hangout staked out. On January 25, one by one, quietly and without gunfire, they arrested the gang. Dillinger and Billie were caught last. At the end of the day, the entire Dillinger gang was in jail.[18]

The news headlines were jubilant. In one fell swoop, without a shot fired, the nation's most feared gang of outlaws had been put behind bars, and Dillinger's run had seemingly come to an end. The authorities were so confident that the Chicago Dillinger Squad was reassigned to other duties. An all-star delegation of law enforcement officials from Ohio and Indiana flew to Arizona to claim jurisdiction over Dillinger—including Matt Leach, the local prosecutor, and a deputy sheriff. They arrived in Tucson to a media circus and couldn't help but get caught up in it. Dillinger had already been charming the local and providing the press with juicy quotes. He was as calm and confident as ever, but things didn't look good for him. After his arrest, the police had found among his possessions bills whose serial number could be linked to the East Chicago heist, and thus to the murder of Officer O'Malley.

While the rest of the gang was flown to Ohio to stand trial for the murder of the officer killed when Dillinger was broken out of the Lima prison, Dillinger himself was taken back to Chicago. He eventually arrived at the Crown Point prison in a 13 car convoy, where another throng of reporters awaited. Dillinger jovially posed with the prison sheriff and the prosecutor, his arm around the prosecutor—a widely circulated photo that would come back to haunt both officials.

Dillinger spent the month of February at Crown Point Prison in Indiana under heavy guard, and his trial was set for March 12. Dillinger hired a high-profile Chicago defense attorney, Louis Piquett, who was also a colorful character; a former bartender, in the early 20s he was Chicago's chief prosecutor until corruption charges forced him to step down. In private practice he represented the full spectrum of the city's organized crime scene, and on the side engaged in questionable stock market deals. His full role in Dillinger's subsequent activities wasn't clear until an unpublished manuscript telling the inside story of Dillinger's escapades was unearthed decades later.[19]

---

[18] Gorn, *Dillinger's Wild Ride*, p. 60
[19] Burroughs, *Public Enemies*, pp. 211-212

One winter day in early 1934, Baby Face Nelson heard again from Homer Van Meter. It seems that Dillinger was now duly impressed with the former two bit hoodlum and had sent Van Meter to personally invite Nelson to join their gang. Of course, it was also convenient timing for Dillinger, who had landed in jail for the third time in 1934 and had lost so many men in recent months that he was interested in merging his gang with Nelson's. Nelson agreed to the merger on one condition: he would call the shots. Much to his own surprise, Van Meter agreed.

Of course, there was still the matter of Dillinger's escape. One of the reasons Dillinger became perhaps the most famous public enemy of the era was his penchant for being captured alive and escaping alive. He had been released on parole in May 1933 after serving nearly 10 years in jail, only to be arrested 3 months later after a bank robbery and sent to jail in Lima, Ohio, where he helped plan the escape of several of his associates just days after landing there. And of course, he had been busted out of there himself in October. He had been in and out of jail seemingly every 3 months.

However, his previous escapades would be child's play compared to Dillinger's legendary escape from Crown Point Prison. On March 3, 1934, a little over a week before his trial was due to begin, the impossible happened: Dillinger, apparently without assistance, escaped from a heavily fortified prison. With just a fake wooden gun he claimed to have whittled himself and then blackened with shoe polish, Dillinger lured one guard, then another, and then another into a holding cell. With the assistance of another prisoner, Herbert Youngblood, Dillinger eventually locked up more than two dozen unarmed prison personnel, including the warden. Then, using Deputy Sheriff Ernest Blunk as a hostage, they raided the prison locker and stocked up on weapons before heading across the street to the city garage. They asked the mechanic for the fastest car, and taking both the mechanic and Blunk as hostages, they sped off, letting the hostages go once they'd put some distance between themselves and the city. Dillinger was once more a free man. Dillinger would even publicly brag about the way he escaped.

In initial newspaper accounts, and even according to many subsequent histories, this was the official story, and it fed into the legend of Dillinger as an endlessly cunning, almost invincible figure. The real story—which emerged slowly as a result of a special investigation by the Indiana attorney general and more skeptical reporters—may have been more complicated, if no less impressive. There is good reason to believe that Dillinger's attorney Louis Piquett and his right-hand man, working in concert with Dillinger's many friends in the criminal underworld, orchestrated the whole thing. Two prison employees, including the deputy sheriff Dillinger took hostage, later came under suspicion, as well as the mechanic. Their theory goes that Piquett was able to smuggle in $5,000 in bribe money, as well the wooden gun, and that Dillinger used the money to buy the cooperation of key prison personnel. But nothing was ever proven, and many both then and now prefer to believe in the initial version of the story.[20]

---

[20] Gorn, *Dillinger's Wild Ride*, pp. 70-80

Regardless of how it actually went down, Dillinger's dramatic escape had profound political consequences. Roosevelt's Attorney General Homer Cummings used the embarrassment to argue for a "New Deal on Crime" that would, among other things, expand the resources and jurisdiction of J. Edgar Hoover's Division of Investigation. Dillinger was once again a free man, but his escape set in motion a major federal effort to ensure that his freedom would be short-lived.

As was often the case with him, Dillinger wasted little time in getting back to work. For one thing, he needed money; arranging his escape had not been cheap, and those funds, not to mention other fees he owed his lawyer, had been borrowed against future earnings. The newly reformed gang gathered in St. Paul this time for a variety of reasons. St. Paul was removed from Chicago, where surveillance would be high, and it was known as a town whose cops could be bought off easily. The gang included Dillinger's old partner Red Hamilton, who had successfully recovered from wounds suffered in East Chicago, as well as Homer Van Meter, a local hood named Eddie Green, the group's driver Tommy Carroll, and Lester Gillis, better known as Baby Face Nelson.

By the time Dillinger had escaped, Baby Face Nelson had developed a name of his own, and he had previously used St. Paul as a hideout. The notoriously violent Baby Face even brought along his family to St. Paul and lived in the elegant Hotel St. Francis there between jobs. Those who encountered him would have never guessed that he was anything other than just another tourist, and he kept the local police sufficiently bribed that no one bothered them.

Things reportedly got off to a rough start when Dillinger arrived in St. Paul to officially meet Baby Face shortly after his escape. To say that the meeting did not go well would be a gross understatement. According to legend, Baby Face led off by announcing that he would be taking orders from no one, not even Dillinger himself. However, the self-confident Dillinger remained cool and continued the conversation, allowing both Nelson and Van Meter, who'd initially gone for their guns, to calm down. Even if it was technically Baby Face leading the gang, everyone outside the gang would continue to believe it was Dillinger leading things.

As if that meeting wasn't enough, the same night Dillinger arrived in town included one of Nelson's worst outbursts. Dillinger and Nelson were on their way to pick up Van Meter when Nelson, who was driving, allegedly got cut off by another driver. Enraged, Nelson began tailing the driver and forced him into a curb. Although no one was hurt, the owner of the other car, a local paint salesman named Theodore Kidder, jumped out and started yelling at Nelson. Nelson responded by pulling out his .45 and shooting Kidder right between the eyes.

But in the eyes of the press and of law enforcement, Dillinger was the key figure.

Only three days after Dillinger's daring escape, the gang hit a bank in Sioux Falls, South Dakota on March 6, 1934. As had happened before, the alarm went off, police were summoned, and a crowd gathered outside—as large as a thousand people, the *New York Times* later claimed. While Tom Carroll waited behind the wheel, the group of robbers strolled into the Security National Bank and Trust Company and shot into the air. Before anyone could blink, one of the employees hit the alarm, sending sirens screaming through the building. Nelson became hysterical and threatened to shoot everyone in the building, while Dillinger firmly ordered him back to his post as look out. Within seconds, motorcycle cop Hale Keith pulled up in front of the building. Upon seeing him, Nelson mowed him down, screaming, "I got one of 'em! I got one of the bastards! That'll teach 'em to interfere!" Though they got away with nearly $50,000, Dillinger was concerned with his uncontrollable new partner, but he realized that breaking ties with Nelson would also mean he would lose Tommy Carroll and Eddie Green, whom he needed and respected. Dillinger decided, for the moment, to keep his new group intact.

A week later they hit another bank in Mason City, Iowa, but the second heist didn't go as smoothly. Dillinger took the precaution of persuading Nelson to drive the getaway car, but things still went haywire. For one thing, the First National Bank in Mason City, Iowa had some new upgrades that Dillinger and his gang were not accustomed to. When Willis Bagley saw some suspicious looking men lurking in the bank lobby, he immediately ran into his office, taking the key to the safe with him and locking the door behind him. Though the robbers fired on the door, it remained solid and kept them out. In the meanwhile, Dillinger discovered that the bank also had a reinforced steel cage in the lobby, through which the guard on duty, Tom Walters, was able to throw tear gas into the main lobby. Eyes stinging and throats burning, the men tried to shoot through the locked cage with no success. Instead, they made their way through the smoke, cleaning out teller drawers and what money could be handed to them through the locked vault bars.

Of course, Nelson knew nothing of this, but he was beginning to get nervous standing out front for so long. By the time Dillinger emerged, John Shipley, a retired police officer working in the office across that street, had realized that something was amiss and had a sniper rifle trained on the sidewalk below. When he saw Dillinger, he fired, catching him in the elbow. Though both Dillinger and Nelson fired back, Shipley remained uninjured.

Seeing he was beaten, Dillinger dashed back into the bank and ordered the rest of the men to the car. Seeing police pulling up at both ends of the street, he also ordered them to bring hostages. As he had in similar situations in the past, Dillinger organized the bank employees into a human shield surrounding him and his men. While the police would not dare to fire, Shipley had a clear shot from his vantage point and took it, shooting through Nelson's hat and hitting Dillinger in the same arm as before. They tried to return fire, but Shipley was out of sight.

By this time Nelson was hysterical. When one of the older hostages failed to move as fast as Nelson thought he should, Nelson prepared to shoot him. However, just before he could get a shot off, Dillinger knocked his gun to the ground, saying calmly, "No need to kill him, Nelson! Now, leave these people be and do your job and get us the hell outta here — and move out easy!" Doing as he was told, the furious Nelson pulled away slowly enough that no hostages were injured. Once they were out of town, Dillinger released them. The gang was forced to leave a lot of money behind, but they had still escaped with another $52,000.

Back in the money, Dillinger took time to plan for the future. In retrospect, some have argued that Dillinger had a death wish, but many of his actions indicate otherwise. He snuck back into Chicago, met with his lawyer, and instructed him to assist his girlfriend Billie in securing a divorce from her estranged husband. He then sent Billie to Mooresville to visit his father and delivery his already legendary wooden gun for safekeeping. The couple reunited in St. Paul where they spent a couple of quiet weeks living under an assumed name.

But that quiet came to an abrupt end on the last day of March. The manager of the apartment building where they'd been staying had grown suspicious and contacted the FBI, leading two FBI agents and a local cop to the apartment to check out the tip. Billie answered the knock on the door and coolly explained that "Mr. Hellman" was out at the moment. They wanted to speak to her instead, and she bought time by asking them to wait outside while she got dressed. This bought time for Dillinger to assemble his submachine gun. In the meantime, Van Meter had arrived at the apartment building, and, sensing something amiss, he stayed downstairs with his weapon drawn. Dillinger opened fire on the agents, who, having to deal with Van Meter firing on them from below, allowed Dillinger and Billie to sneak out the back. It was another narrow escape for Dillinger and another embarrassment for the FBI.[21]

Although he had gotten away yet again, Dillinger had been hit in the leg by one of his bullets as it ricocheted off something during the gunfight. He got treatment from a doctor (who would later be imprisoned for helping him) and recuperated in an apartment Eddie Green arranged for him. J. Edgar Hoover, furious not only that Dillinger had again slipped away but that he had opened fire on two of his agents, made the outlaw the agency's top priority and put Melvin Purvis in charge of the effort. Purvis was given nearly 50 men, and together they scoured St. Paul and eventually tracked down and arrested Green's wife Bessie as she picked up some of Dillinger's things in the apartment. Though Dillinger was long gone, her arrest and questioning turned up important leads that would eventually bear fruit.

---

[21] Burroughs, *Public Enemies*, p.271

Hoover

On April 3, federal agents made their first major hit against the gang when they ambushed and killed Eddie Green. After that, the rest of the gang dispersed. Baby Face Nelson returned to Reno, where he came to the aid of two old friends, Bill Graham and Jim McKay. Graham and McKay were on trial for federal mail fraud, so Nelson kidnapped and killed the chief witness against them, Roy Fritch, tossing his dead and mutilated body down a mine shaft.

Meanwhile, in a risky move, Dillinger headed home to Mooresville for what would turn out to be one last visit with his father and family. Though he arrived at night and took other precautions, he stayed for several days, and many in town knew of his presence but chose not to share the information with authorities. During the stay, Dillinger posed for a picture that would become one of the most famous shots of the outlaw, holding his wooden gun with one hand and a submachine gun in the other as he stood in the backyard of his father's house. Why the Dillinger house wasn't already being monitored isn't exactly clear, but once again Dillinger's timing was uncanny. Shortly after he departed town, the houses of his father, sister, and brother were all raided by police. Of course, the news that Dillinger had dared to openly visit his family for a few days only added to his legend.

Dillinger with the wooden gun and submachine gun

Dillinger had eluded authorities, but the net was tightening. A week later, Dillinger and his girlfriend were in Chicago, and, as was standard procedure, Billie made inquiries about a temporary hideout for the couple. She was in a bar meeting one of Dillinger's underworld contacts while he waited safely in the car when someone tipped off the FBI, and a group of agents quickly arrived and arrested Billie. It was a breakthrough for the FBI, but also an embarrassment, since Dillinger had been there for the taking but once again slipped away.

By mid-April, the various members of the gang had come back to the Midwest. Baby Face Nelson and his wife Helen were hiding out in a cabin in Iron County, Wisconsin, and according to legend he pouted because Dillinger was Public Enemy Number One instead of him. To make matters worse, Hoover was offering a reward of $20,000 dollars for Dillinger's death, but only half that for Nelson.

Despite the heat and close calls, by the middle of that month Dillinger and Nelson felt it was safe enough to get back together and begin to plan some jobs. Accompanied by their wives and girlfriends, they checked into the isolated Little Bohemia Lodge in Wisconsin at the recommendation of Louis Piquett, who assured them it was a quiet, out of site location where Dillinger could nurse his injured arm in peace. The innkeeper, Emil Wanatka, welcomed the men as friends of a good customer, but he did not know who he was dealing with until later Friday night. That night, during a poker game, he noticed that his guests were all wearing side arms under the coats.

Little Bohemia Lodge

Wanatka mentioned this situation to his wife but decided to take a "don't ask, don't tell" attitude to his guest's identities. His wife, however, was intrigued by their glamorous and dangerous customers. The next day, she took their four year old son to a birthday party where she confided to her brother-in-law, Henry Voss, that she was nervous about having them there. He in turn informed the FBI, who sent their best team of agents, led by Purvis and Sam Cowley.

Upon arriving in Wisconsin, the more than 35 agents learned that the gang looked like they were preparing to move out. Concerned about losing their prey, they moved in quickly and without requesting back up from local law enforcement. This proved to be a mistake. First, two of the cars they were riding in broke down, forcing the agents to ride on the running boards of the remaining cars the rest of the way to the lodge. Then, unknown to them, they had come on one of the restaurant's few crowded nights, when the owner offered a popular dollar special. Seeing a 1933 Chevy coupe leaving, the agents ordered the occupants to halt. When they didn't, they thought they had their men and sprayed the car with bullets, killing innocent customer

Eugene Boisneau and wounding John Hoffman and John Morris. Morris and Hoffman would later explain that they never heard the order because they had the car radio on.

At that moment, gang member Pat Reilly pulled up with his girlfriend, Pat Cherrington. Seeing the agents, they managed to escape in the confusion. Likewise, Dillinger, Van Meter, Carroll and Hamilton went out the back door, which the FBI officers had failed to secure. After moving through the woods on foot, the four split up, stole a couple of cars and drove off into the night, leaving Nelson to face the cops alone.

This predicament didn't seem to bother Baby Face. Coming out of his cabin shooting, he exchanged fire with several agents before making his way into the lodge. There he made his way out the back door, just as his partners had, but he took off in the opposite direction. When he finally made his way out of the dense woods, he was about a mile from the lodge and at the home of a couple named Lange, whom he kidnapped and ordered to drive him away. When Mr. Lange didn't drive fast enough to suit him, Nelson ordered him to pull over so that he could drive. Whether Lange meant to or not, he pulled up in front of the home of local switchboard operator Alvin Koerner, who had already heard about what was going on and called authorities to tell them that he had one of the gangsters in his front yard.

Just as Koerner hung up, Nelson burst through the door and ordered Koerner to freeze. Moments later, the innkeeper Wanatka and two other men arrived at the house to check on Koerner. Nelson also took them hostage. Unbeknownst to him, however, a fourth man had remained hidden in the back seat of their car. Nelson ordered Wanatka and Koerner into the car, not noticing the fourth man in the back seat. Wanatka took the wheel and prepared to drive off, but before he could put the car in gear, two federal agents and a local constable arrived. Not realizing what they were getting themselves into, they let Baby Face get the drop on them. He ordered them from their car but then opened fire, killing Agent Carter Baum and wounding Agent Jay Newman and Constable Carl Christensen.

With the agents out of the way, Nelson jumped into their car and sped off, but even now he wasn't in the clear. Before he could get far a tire blew out and the car became stuck in the mud. Unable to get to the tire to change it, Nelson took off on foot through the woods and came upon the cabin of a Native American family, whom he stayed with for several days before stealing their car and driving off.

Much to Nelson's dismay, Helen and two other women were captured by the FBI at the lodge. Though they questioned all three extensively, they could find no evidence of any serious wrongdoing on anyone's part. After charging them with harboring fugitives from the law, the police released them on parole, probably hoping that the women would lead them back to the fugitives.

In total, the incident at Little Bohemia left one agent and one innocent citizen dead, two agents and two citizens wounded, and the Dillinger gang unscathed. Needless to say, the public was not happy. Some were calling for Hoover to resign, while others insisted the agent Purvis, who headed up the fiasco, be fired. To deflect criticism from himself and his team, Hoover emphasized to the public the sacrifice of the brave, heroic Agent Baum, who had given his life protecting theirs, and reassured everyone that he would not rest until Baum's killer was brought to justice.[22]

The gang had slipped by the FBI at Little Bohemia in several groups and that was how they escaped. Dillinger, Hamilton and Van Meter stole a car from another nearby lodge and made their way back to St. Paul. They circled around the town and came in from the south, thinking that would be safer, but local police recognized the reported license plate and gave pursuit. A gunfight broke out and Hamilton was mortally wounded, but Dillinger and Van Meter escaped to Aurora, Illinois.

Dillinger was out of sight for much of the next two months. He and Van Meter engaged in a relatively small heist on May 2 just outside of Toledo which netted $17,000, more than enough to tide them over for a while. For weeks they lived in an abandoned shack outside of East Chicago, and then they lived in their truck, sleeping on a mattress in the back by night and driving the backroads by day.

It was on those Indiana back roads that they made their second noteworthy public appearance in May. In an incident on May 24 about which there are wildly conflicting reports, their truck was approached by two plainclothes East Chicago detectives. With Dillinger at the wheel, Van Meter opened fire at the men and killed them both. Subsequent accounts suggest the two detectives may have been set up by a fellow officer, Martin Zarkovich. Zarkovich, who had repeatedly fallen under suspicion for corruption, had also been seen at the Crown Point prison while Dillinger was there. The theory goes that he had some involvement in Dillinger's breakout and wanted the detectives, who knew about ongoing bribing of the East Chicago force, eliminated.[23]

Regardless, Dillinger and Van Meter knew they had to get off the roads after that, and they eventually settled down for most of the month of June in a seedy apartment on the far North Side owned by an associate of Dillinger's lawyer. There they came up with a plan to disappear even more completely. Dillinger had for a while entertained the notion of disguising himself through plastic surgery. He finally prevailed upon his lawyer to hook him up with a couple of doctors of questionable character who agreed for a fee of $5,000 to conduct the surgery, first for him, then for Van Meter. The operation wasn't exactly a success. Their crude methods of anesthesia nearly killed Dillinger, and even after a long bloody operation, the outlaw was still mostly recognizable despite the removal of several moles, a building up of the nose, and a filling in of his chin

---

[22] Burroughs, *Public Enemies,* Chapter 12
[23] Gorn, *Dillinger's Wild Ride,* pp. 131-132

dimple. And despite the issues with Dillinger's operation, Van Meter went ahead with his own operation. The two men also had their fingerprints removed.[24]

In spite of the absence of real news about Dillinger over these two months, America's Public Enemy Number One hardly disappeared from the news. If anything, Dillinger's low profile only added to his legend. An endless stream of articles appeared on the FBI's debacle at Little Bohemia, and Dillinger "sightings" came in from around the country. At the end of June, Dillinger celebrated his 31st birthday, and though his surgery scars were still healing, he actually began spending time in public. He attended baseball games at Wrigley Field during the day and went to clubs at night. With his previous girl Billie having been convicted the month before, he even found a new girlfriend, Polly Hamilton.

While Van Meter remained more cautious, the plastic surgery apparently emboldened Dillinger and gave him hope that he was still invincible. As in the Hollywood movies that his life sometimes seemed to resemble, Dillinger dreamed of one last big score, after which he would ride off into the sunset and disappear for good in Mexico, Latin America or some other exotic locale. On June 30, Nelson, Dillinger and Van Meter held up the Merchants National Bank in South Bend, Indiana. Helping them may have been another Public Enemy, Pretty Boy Floyd, although that has never been proven conclusively. Regardless, the robbery began badly and only got worse. Van Meter immediately shot and killed the first police officer on the scene, Howard Wagner. Then Nelson was fired on by a local jeweler, Harry Berg, who hit him in the chest. However, Nelson's bulletproof vest kept him from being seriously injured, and their exchange of shots wounded an innocent bystander. In the ensuing chaos, an unarmed teenaged boy named Joseph Pawlowski tackled Van Meter, who hit him over the head with his gun.

Meanwhile, Dillinger and his accomplices ran out of the bank carrying about $28,000 and bringing along three hostages. Undeterred by dangers to the civilians, the police still fired, wounding two of the hostages and grazing Van Meter's head. Though several other citizens were wounded in the melee, the police did accomplish what they set out to do: neither Dillinger nor Nelson would ever rob another bank.

Tired of being away from the city's nightlife, Dillinger moved from the seedy apartment at the edge of town to an apartment run by Anna Sage, a former prostitute who now had her own brothel and had in fact introduced Dillinger to his new girlfriend. Dillinger and Polly lived it up over the next few weeks, and Dillinger's extreme confidence and risk-taking seem to have been rooted in a plan he and Van Meter were brainstorming. They had been developing a plan to ambush and rob a mail train. Using nitroglycerine, they would blow open the train's armored car and walk away with their biggest score ever. The plan so captured their imagination, they even began talking about writing a screenplay detailing their exploits.[25]

---

[24] Burroughs, *Public Enemies*, Chapter 14
[25] Gorn, *Dillinger's Wild Ride,* p.141

The line between reality and the movies was blurring. And in an entirely fitting way, that theme of unreality marked Dillinger's end. Even while he and Van Meter were plotting their grand plan, a plot to bring the famous outlaw down was falling into place. Anna Sage was facing serious legal troubles. She was a Romanian immigrant facing deportation by the U.S. Immigration Service, as well as new prostitution charges. She brokered a deal with the Feds, mediated by none other than Martin Zarkovich, the corrupt East Chicago cop who also happened to be her boyfriend. She told the Feds that she was going to the movies with Dillinger and Polly Hamilton the next night, and that she would be wearing an orange dress so that the authorities could spot her. Though she was unsure which theater they were going to, she told them it would either be the Biograph Theater or the Marbro.

On the night of July 22, Sage accompanied Dillinger and his girlfriend to the movies. Ironically, the film they attended was *Manhattan Melodrama*, the story of a gangster played by Clark Gable who ends up going to the electric chair for his life of crime. Meanwhile, the Feds were waiting outside both the Biograph Theater and the Marbro Theater, so conspicuous that the Biograph's manager actually called the Chicago police on them, thinking they were criminals casing the place. When the Chicago police arrived, the Feds had to wave them away.

Led by Melvin Purvis, the agents waited outside the theater, having decided it would be best to take Dillinger down as he left the film. As the film ended and customers came out, Purvis signaled Dillinger's exit by lighting his cigar while standing at the entrance. Somehow, Dillinger got the sense that something was wrong; after making eye contact with Purvis, Dillinger stepped out ahead of the two women and tried but failed to grab his gun. As agents approached him and ordered him to surrender, Dillinger tried to flee into an alley, only to find that federal agents had closed that escape off. At least three agents fired several rounds at Dillinger, hitting Dillinger in the back and sending him face first to the pavement. Dillinger had been hit three or four times, with the fatal shot having gone through the back of his neck and out his head just below his right eye, killing him instantly. The man credited with firing the fatal shot, Charles Winstead, would be given a personal letter of commendation from Hoover himself.

The apparently invincible outlaw Houdini who had slipped away so many times had finally met his end.[26]

---

[26] Gorn, *Dillinger's Wild Ride*, pp. 142-145

The Biograph Theater in 1934

Dillinger's legend only grew with his death, and the myth-making began almost from the moment his body hit the sidewalk. A huge crowd gathered that night, scavenging for souvenirs and hoping for a glimpse of the dead outlaw. As people around the theater began to realize what had just happened and who the target was, some of them dipped their handkerchief in the famous outlaw's blood. Crowds followed Dillinger as his body made its way, first to the hospital where he was declared dead, then to the coroner's office, and finally to a funeral home in Mooresville. Rumors began circulating about a "lady in red" who had betrayed Dillinger. The coroner's office returned a mere seven dollars to Dillinger's father, and another set of rumors grew about what had happened to all of the outlaw's money. Still more rumors flew around about Dillinger's brain having been removed during the autopsy.

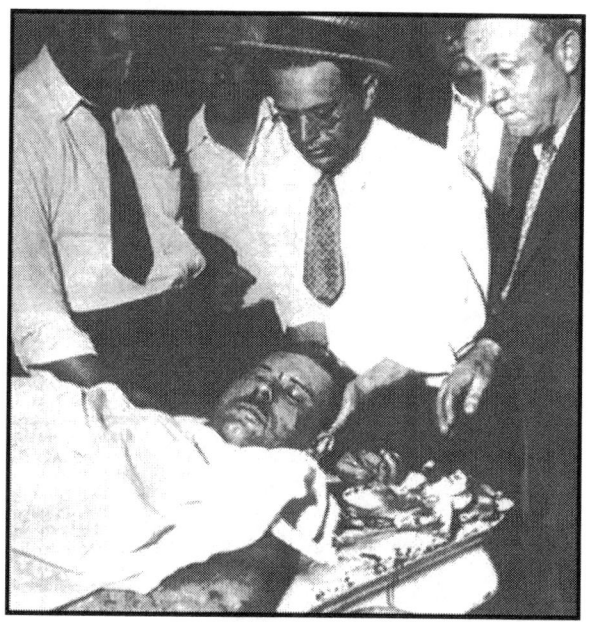

Dillinger's body

Of course, like Jesse James and other famous outlaws, rumors that Dillinger had somehow escaped or not been killed outside the theater persisted. Author Jay Nash has extensively argued in his book, *The Dillinger Dossier*, that the man killed outside the Biograph Theater that night was not Dillinger but another petty thief known as Jimmy Lawrence, who slightly resembled Dillinger. Nash's theory was that Martin Zarkovich set up the elaborate plot to have someone take the fall in Dillinger's place, which would allow Dillinger to escape the heat, and that the FBI covered it up upon realizing that they had killed someone other than Dillinger. According to his elaborate conspiracy, Nash insisted Dillinger was still alive and well, living out his life doing manual labor in California.

J. Edgar Hoover carefully nurtured his official version of the Dillinger story. Shortly after the outlaw's death, Van Meter and Nelson and other famous Depression-era bandits were captured or killed, lending credence to Hoover's claim that the new federal War on Crime was bearing fruit and reversing the tide. The following year, his Division of Investigation was renamed the FBI, and the hunt for Dillinger was front and center in the new agency's own history of itself. In his office, Hoover installed an exhibit case holding an array of Dillinger memorabilia, including the hat and glasses the outlaw was wearing the night he was killed. Up to this day, FBI trainees engaged in target practice sometimes shoot at life-sized John Dillinger targets. Over the years,

Hoover carefully turned the outlaw into a symbol of his agency's triumph and a moral lesson that crime does not pay.[27]

Chapter 7: The Battle of Barrington

With the most famous outlaw of them all now dead, Pretty Boy Floyd became Public Enemy Number One on July 23. Then, Van Meter was killed in St. Paul, Minnesota by police a few weeks later, leaving Nelson the sole survivor of the original gang. Floyd was killed the following October, putting Baby Face in his much coveted Public Enemy Number One Position. By this time, the Nelsons and Chase had gone back out west, moving from place to place in California and Nevada. They then returned to Chicago in November, moving into the Lake Como Inn in Lake Geneva, Wisconsin.

Nelson might have lived on had he stayed in hiding, but it was clear that he and Dillinger simply could not stand inactivity for long periods of time. Instead, he began to make noises around town about looking for some new men to help him start another bank robbing enterprise. By now, however, he found no one was interested in working for him. His reputation as a loose cannon preceded him, and even the most hardened criminals were reluctant to get involved with a man who had a tendency to shoot it out with cops than slip away quietly with the loot.

By November 1934, Cowley and Purvis were trying to track Nelson's every move and were closing in on him. They knew that he was somewhere in the Chicago area and were determined to find him. In order to do so, they had as many men as they could assign patrolling all the major highways outside the city, traveling up and down the road looking for Nelson, whom they were all trained to recognize.

On November 27, 1934, their hard work finally paid off. Federal agents William Ryan and Thomas McDade caught up with Nelson, Chase and Helen in front of a gas station just north of Chicago. As it turned out, Nelson had also been doing his homework; he had compiled a list of license plates used by police and federal agents, which allowed him to recognize cars and even try to attack them. Thus, when Agents Ryan and McDade recognized Nelson while driving the other way down the road, he also recognized them as agents. Both cars did U-turns to try to chase each other, and in a strange twist of fate, it was Nelson who started chasing the agents.

During the chase, the agents exchanged fire with Nelson and Chase, whose shots had shattered the agents' windshields. For their part, the agents radioed to their bosses and Ryan fired a shot that destroyed the radiator of Nelson's Ford. Just as bullets rendered the agents' car useless, Sam Cowley and Herman Hollis picked up the trail.

---

[27] Powers, *G-Men*, pp. 114-115

FBI's photograph of Agent Hollis, who was credited with firing the fatal shot that killed Pretty Boy Floyd a month earlier

Due to the damage inflicted by the agents on Nelson's car, he swerved the car into the entrance of Barrington's North Side Park as Hollis and Cowley went driving past him. As the outlaws fired at the federal agents and Helen ran for an open field to escape, Hollis and Cowley slid their car in nearby and took cover behind it. Expecting a gun battle with each car acting as a fortress, the agents were shocked to see Nelson walking toward them, firing his .351 rifle so many times in succession that bystanders would later incorrectly believe he had a machine gun. As Nelson exposed himself, the agents hit him multiple times with submachine gun fire. However, Chase was still firing from the protection of the outlaws' car, and Nelson somehow summoned the strength to sit up on the running board of the car and keep pumping shots at the agents, eventually mortally wounding Cowley while Hollis's shotgun blasted him in the legs. Even still, Nelson kept getting up, and as he did so Hollis tried to move behind a utility pole, only to catch a bullet in the head.

With Hollis all but dead and Cowley mortally wounded, Nelson somehow staggered to his feet and made his way to the agents' now bullet-riddled car. Chase hurried over and got behind the wheel, and the two scooped up Helen and fled the scene. Hollis was dead on arrival, and Cowley would die the next day after unsuccessful surgery.

The fact that Nelson was still alive as the outlaws fled was miraculous; he had been shot 17 times, with seven submachine gun bullets hitting him in the chest and 10 shotgun pellets ripping into his legs. Chase drove them to a safe house in Wilmette, Illinois, but as Nelson told his wife,

"I'm done for." He died in bed at the safehouse that same evening. Chase would eventually be apprehended and sent to Alcatraz.

A local newspaper gave a rather terse description of the battle, emphasizing the importance of the officers, rather than the criminals.

"Special Agent Samuel Cowley and Special Agent Herman Hollis were shot and killed by the infamous gangster Baby Face Nelson near Barrington, Illinois.

When two other agents had encountered Baby Face Nelson, his wife, Helen Gillis, and a male companion, John Paul Chase, driving down a road, a gun battle ensued as both parties recognized each other. The agent's, with their windshields shattered, were forced off the road into a field but not before they had disabled the suspect's car.

As Agents Hollis and Cowley approached the scene and exited their car, they were met with gunfire by both male suspects. Agent Hollis, with massive head wounds, was pronounced dead upon arrival at a hospital and Agent Cowley died the following morning after surgery for his stomach wounds.

The suspects fled the scene in the agent's car and drove to a house in Wilmette. Baby Face Nelson, who had been shot nine times, died there later that evening. His body was discovered wrapped in a blanket in a ditch in front of a cemetery in Skokie. He had also been responsible for the murder of Special Agent W. Carter Baum seven months earlier."

A few weeks later, after Helen Gillis had been taken into custody, the *New York Times* sent a reporter to her sister's home, where they received a different take on the events of that day.

"Mrs. Fitzsimmons reveled to newspaper men that Mrs. Nelson had told her that she, Nelson and the other man were in a cottage near Lake Geneva, Wisconsin, for ten days until a raid by Federal men a week ago yesterday, when they fled out the back door and escaped in a car.

On the way to Chicago, she related, they sped safely through one Federal trap, in which several shots were fired, and then raced on to encounter Cowley and Hollis near Barrington.

'The Federal men's fire disabled our automobile,' Mrs. Fitzsimmons quoted the widow as saying. 'I could almost feel the bullets as they whistled past my face.'

Following that, Nelson, the unidentified man and Mrs. Nelson leaped from the car.

'Les hollered at me to duck and I jumped into a ditch and kept my head down,' the widow was quoted as saying. 'I could see Les firing back at the Federal men who were trying to kill him.'

'A few seconds after the firing started I could see Les jump up and grab his side. I seemed to know that it was over. I was in that ditch until the firing stopped.'

She said the three fugitives climbed into the Federal car. Nelson attempted to drive, but was too weak, and the other man took the wheel, Mrs. Nelson said to her sister-in-law.

She said they found their way to a house "somewhere near Chicago," into which they carried Nelson, stripped him of his clothing and attempted to care for his machine gun wounds.

'All three of us knew Les was dying,' the widow was quoted as saying. Later, she said, he told her to say good-bye for him to their two children.

At 7:35 that evening, three hours after the battle, she said, Nelson died, and they took the body to a point near Niles Center.

'We placed his body on the grass,' Mrs. Nelson was quoted as saying. 'I covered him with a blanket and tucked it around him because he always hated the cold weather.'"

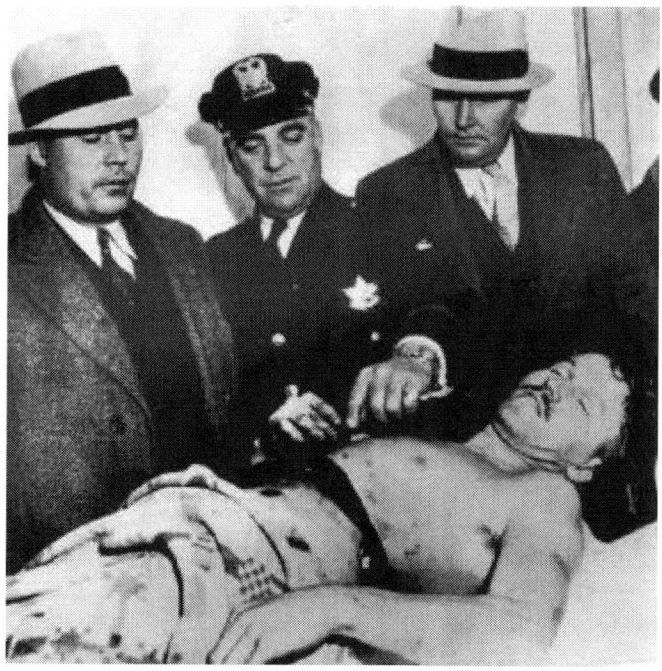

Authorities surround Baby Face Nelson's body

Today Baby Face Nelson remains yet another name on a short list of criminals who rose to fame during the Thirties. While he aspired to be like the handsome, dashing John Dillinger, he was simply too volatile to emulate Dillinger or capture the public's attention in the same way as his cool, calm, and collected partner. While his wife certainly grieved for him, as did his two young children and John Chase, most of the rest of his underworld associates breathed a sigh of relief when he was gone. While they respected Dillinger for his calm, well thought-out planning and relatively less violent demeanor, they despised Nelson's flamboyance and cockiness. No matter how many times he was told, he could never understand that his love of unnecessary violence brought too much attention to other criminals who were just out to make a buck.

Of course, it seems obvious now that making money was never at the heart of what Nelson did. In his mind, making a name for himself, trying to get respect to make up for those who had tormented him as a child, was always more important. In that sense, he got what he wanted. By running with Dillinger and being Public Enemy Number One himself, America has not forgotten Baby Face Nelson. And if anything, the glamorization of his contemporaries, from gangsters like Al Capone to outlaws like Dillinger and Bonnie & Clyde, have allowed Baby Face Nelson to be lumped in by association with those who were more captivating and level-headed.

Chapter 8: The Dillinger Gang's Impact

If Dillinger's life often seemed to resemble a Hollywood movie, Hollywood went on to play a major role in his ongoing legacy. The movie industry underwent a profound shift in the early '30s. Films that openly romanticized flashy urban gangsters like Al Capone had been a mainstay of Hollywood in the '20s, but in response to public fear and revulsion of crime in the Depression, the industry imposed on itself a strict code that would remain in place for two decades, one that banned glorification of violence and sex. For a brief period of a couple of years, however, explicit violence was allowed if the purpose of the film was to denounce criminality and extoll the virtues of law enforcement.

During this transitional period, the public got their fill of movie violence in films that romanticized not criminals but those who sought to put them behind bars, particularly the agents of the newly revitalized FBI. Emblematic of this shift was the actor James Cagney, who appeared as a gangster in the 1932 film *Public Enemies*, only to reappear as a federal agent in the 1935 film *G-Men* (short for "Government Men," popular slang designating FBI agents).

As the Hollywood Code of the '30s eventually fell into disrepute and became outdated, movies exploring the grit and grime of criminal life began reappearing. Gangster films started making a comeback in the '50s, and Dillinger himself has naturally popped up in every decade. Some of his more notable appearances include Warren Oates in the title role of a 1973 film, Robert Conrad in 1979's *The Lady in Red*, and Johnny Depp in Michael Mann's 2009 *Public Enemies*.

Dillinger has remained a pop culture fixture since his spree and demise, but his life and death had an important impact on the real world as well. The wave of bank robberies for which the '30s were famous was most heavily concentrated in the struggling farm states of the Midwest, and J. Edgar Hoover would go so far as to call the tri-state area comprising Kansas, Missouri and Oklahoma the "crime corridor." As early as 1930, a bank raid in this region was a weekly occurrence, more often than not followed by a car chase.

As urban banks fortified themselves with updated security measures, bandits turned toward more vulnerable rural banks. In addition to featuring less formidable security, rural banks allowed outlaws to quickly disappear into the countryside via a vast network of newly paved roads. While bank robbers such as Dillinger might have been embraced as folk heroes by some, this was not the case among the rural townspeople of the Midwest. As more and more banks in the region fell victim to well-organized heists, locals began forming "citizen protective associations" to supplement bank security. Informal posses sometimes sped off in pursuit of fleeing getaway cars, often at great personal risk.[28] Dillinger's gang had come across vigilantes on a handful of occasions, and his success ensured that such a system stayed in place.

In recent years, some historians contend that the crime wave of the early '30s was more a product of perception than of reality.[29] What these historians argue is with society apparently crumbling around them, the American public saw outlaws like John Dillinger, and the spectacular crimes they committed, in highly symbolic terms. As one historian puts it, "every major crime was turned into a test of whether America and its values could survive the depression."[30] Amidst such a fearful environment, the federal government actively encouraged this perception, in a sense "marketing" outlaws and promoting them as celebrities. They did so to justify the passage of an ambitious package of anti-crime legislation that radically redefined the role of the federal government in law enforcement. The War on Crime that emerged from this legislation served two purposes. First, it reassured an anxious public desperate for a semblance of order and normalcy. Second, it paved the way for aggressive federal intervention in other areas of American life as well.

A look at the historical record provides some evidence for this view. The FBI didn't collect national crime statistics until 1930, and even then the records were sketchy until 1933. But examinations of crime trends in various cities suggest that "serious crime in America rose to a peak in 1918 and steadily declined until the 1940s."[31]

But if the actual crime wave of the 1930s was a subjective matter, the public reaction to that perceived crime wave was all too real. After the Lindbergh kidnapping in 1932, an editorial in the *New York Herald Tribune* declared that an "army of desperate criminals which has been recruited in the last decade is winning its battle against society." Other papers calls for citizen

---

[28] Potter, *War on Crime*, pp. 69-72
[29] among others: Claire Bond Potter, *War on Crime;* and Richard Powers, *G-Men*
[30] Powers, *G-Men*, p. xv
[31] Powers, *G-Men*, p.295

vigilante groups, an American version of Scotland Yard, even nationalization of the police. The first use of the term "Public Enemy" to describe a criminal was by the Chicago Crime Commission, a private gathering of lawyers, bankers, and businessmen that had gone as far as hiring its own investigators to seek punishment for high-profile criminals. The public, and the culture, were demanding action. The popular "Dick Tracy" cartoon strip pre-dated the actual War on Crime by several years. When Attorney General Homer Cummings finally assembled his national Conference on Crime, it was a belated response to a swelling of public opinion long in the making.[32]

Much has been made of the contrast between the urban gangsters of the 20s and the rural outlaws of the 30s. There were indeed some real differences; Al Capone and other gangsters of the Roaring Twenties saw themselves as businessmen trying, in their own way, to become part of and take advantage of the system—a system that was viewed by many as offering everyone a real the chance of prosperity. By contrast, John Dillinger and other Depression-era outlaws saw themselves as enemies of the system at a time when that system seemed to be failing the majority. But the contrast between outlaws and gangsters can be overdrawn. Dillinger and other outlaws spent considerable time in jail before embarking on their crime sprees, and while in prison they came into contact with established figures of organized crime who would prove to be key allies once they were released. In between their notorious bank heists, outlaws needed a place to lay low, and they frequently made use of the brothels and clubs controlled by organized crime.[33] They also used their underworld contacts to obtain weapons and to get rid of stolen goods. It is no accident that the supposed farm boy John Dillinger spent his final days and met his end on the streets of Chicago.

Bibliography

Burroughs, Bryan. *Public Enemies.* New York: The Penguin Press, 2004

Borus, Daniel H. (ed.) These United States — Portraits of America From the 1920s. Ithaca, NY: Cornell University Press, 1992.

Cromie, Ronert and Pinkston, Joseph. *Dillinger: A Short And Violent Life.* Chicago Historical Bookworks, 1962.

Gorn, Elliott J. *Dillinger's Wild Ride.* New York: Oxford University Press, 2009

Kennedy, David. *Freedom From Fear.* New York: Oxford University Press, 2001

Lindberg, Richard. Return to the Scene of the Crime. Nashville, TN: Cumberland House, 1999.

---

[32] Powers, *G-Men,* Chapter 2
[33] Potter, *War on Crime,* p. 86

Nash, Jay Robert. Bloodletters and Badmen. NY: M. Evans & Company, Inc., 1995.

Nickel, Steven; William J. Helmer. Baby Face Nelson: Portrait of a Public Enemy. Cumberland House Publishing, 2002.

Potter, Claire Bond. *War on Crime*. New Brunswick: Rutgers University Press, 1998

Powers, Richard Gid. *G-Men*. Carbondale & Edwardsville: Southern Illinois University Press, 1983

Wallis, Michael Pretty Boy. NY: St. Martin's Press, 1992.

William, J. Helmer. Baby Face Nelson. Cumberland House, 2002.

Zion, Sidney. Loyalty and Betrayal — The Story of the American Mob. San Francisco: Collins Publishers, 1994.

Bonnie & Clyde

Chapter 1: A Girl Named Bonnie

> "You've heard of a woman's glory
> Being spent on a "downright cur"
> Still you can't always judge the story
> As true, being told by her." – Bonnie Parker, "The Trail's End"

Bonnie and a 1932 Ford V-8 B-400 convertible sedan. The picture was found by lawmen in Joplin while the Barrow Gang was on the run.

Bonnie Elizabeth Parker was born on October 1, 1910 in Rowena, Texas to parents who were a typical middle-class American family of that era. Bonnie was the middle child of the family, along with Buster, who was older than Bonnie, and Billie Jean, who was born two years later. When Bonnie was four, her father Charles died, leaving Bonnie's mother Emma a poor widow with three young children. In order to survive, she left Rowena and moved in with her parents in a Dallas suburb known as Cement City.

From all appearances, Bonnie was a happy, well-adjusted child who did well in school. She won several academic honors in high school and was particularly adept at writing and public speaking. America would soon learn all about her writing abilities, as the outlaw spent some of her time writing poems about her exploits, including the prophetic "The Trail's End," better known as "The Story of Bonnie and Clyde".

In her sophomore year, Bonnie met a rough character named Roy Thornton. Much to her family's dismay she left high school and married him on September 25, 1926, days before her 16th birthday. Not surprisingly, the marriage proved to be a disaster, as Thornton spent much of his time dodging the law and often left his very young wife on her own for days at a time. Bonnie left him in January of 1929 but never filed for divorce. Though Bonnie would forever be associated with another man, she was wearing Thornton's wedding ring when she died, and by that point Thornton was in jail himself. Though they were no longer together, he had followed his wife's exploits with interest and told a reporter ruefully, "I'm glad they went out like they did. It's much better than being caught." Thornton would be killed in an attempted prison escape in 1937.

Thornton

Following her separation from Thornton, Bonnie moved back in with her mother and took a job as a waitress in Dallas. She was a pretty girl at that time. She had an oval face and fair skin, which she accented by bright lipstick. She wore her auburn hair bobbed and curled on the ends. Her thin figure (her wanted poster said she was 5 foot 5 inches tall and weighed only 100 pounds) was well suited for the short, flapper style dresses of the 20s.

One of her most frequent customers was Ted Hinton, a postal worker who would soon join the Dallas Sheriff's Office and, just a few years later, fire some of the bullets that killed her. But that day was still a few years off, and Bonnie was just a friendly young waitress trying to survive in a seedy part of Dallas. She briefly kept a diary during these early years and her turbulent marriage to Thornton, in which she wrote a nearly heart wrenching account of her loneliness, still so young and yet already feeling used up by life:

Dear Diary,

Before opening this year's diary I wish to tell you that I have a roaming husband with a roaming mind. We are separated again for the third and last time. The first time, August 9-19,1927; and the second time, October 1-19, 1927; and the third time, December 5, 1927. I love him very much and miss him terribly. But I intend doing my duty. I am not going to take him back. I am running around with Rosa Mary Judy and she is somewhat a consolation to me. We have resolved this New Year's to take no men or nothing seriously. Let all men go to hell! But we are not going to sit back and let the world sweep by us.

January 1, 1928. New Year's nite. 12:00 The bells are ringing, the old year has gone, and my heart has gone with it. I have been the happiest and most miserable woman this last year. I wish the old year would have taken my past with it. I mean all my memories, but I can't forget Roy. I am very blue tonight. No word from him. I feel he has gone for good. This is New Years Day, Jan. 1. I went to a show. Saw Ken Maynard in The Overland Stage. Am very blue. Well, I must confess this New Years nite I got drunk, trying to forget. Drowning my sorrows in bottled hell.

January 2, 1928. Met Rosa Mary today and we went to a show. Saw Ronald Coleman and Vilma Banky in A Night Of Love. Sure was a good show. Saw Scottie and gave him the air. He's a pain in the neck to me. Came home at 5:30. went to bed at 10:30. Sure am lonesome."

Her only way out of these feelings of despair lay in regular visits to the local movie theater, where, lost in the dark, she could indulge in dreams of a better, more exciting life. She mentioned some of the movies she saw, including *Framed* (starring Milton Sills), *Afraid to Love* (starring Clive Brook and Florence Vidor), *Marriage* starring (Virginia Valli), and *The Primrose Path* (starring Clara Bow).

Chapter 2: A Boy Named Clyde

> "They call them cold-blooded killers
> They say they are heartless and mean
> But I say this with pride, I once knew Clyde
> When he was honest and upright and clean.
>
> But the laws fooled around and taking him down
> and locking him up in a cell
> 'Til he said to me, "I'll never be free,
> So I'll meet a few of them in hell." – Bonnie Parker, "The Trail's End"

Clyde Chestnut Barrow was born on March 24, 1909 in Ellis County, Texas, joining four older siblings born to Henry Basil and Cumie Walker Barrow. The senior Barrows were poor farmers and would go on to have seven more children before moving, a few at a time, to West Dallas, something of a slum, during the early 1920s. The family was so poor that they spent their first few months in town living under their wagon while saving up money to buy a tent.

In 1926, Clyde, longing to experience the way the "other half" lived, rented a car for a joy ride around the countryside. The problem was, he decided not to return it. His mugshot from that incident shows a young, clean cut looking boy of 16, with dark eyes and slightly pointed ears. It looks more like it belongs to a kid running for class treasurer than a future murderer. However, the class treasury was not the money that Clyde wanted to control.

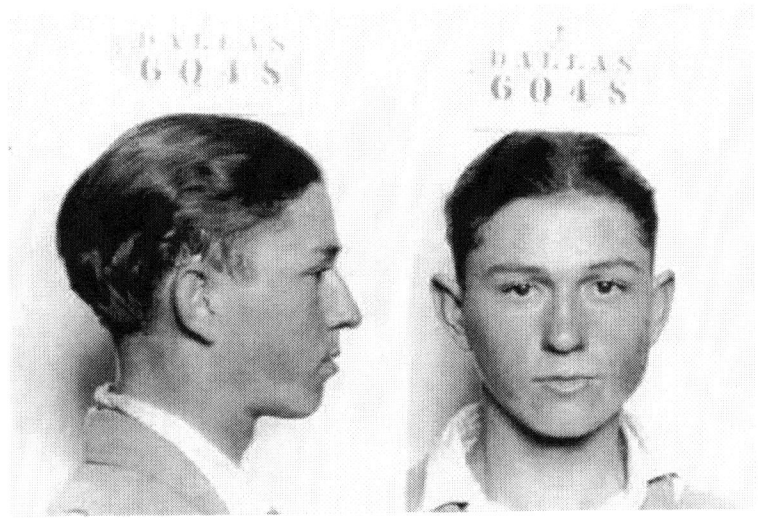

Before many months passed, Clyde was arrested again when he and his brother Buck stole some turkeys. They were not convicted, probably due to their poverty and age, and they soon obtained paying jobs. Nevertheless, they persisted in augmenting their meager honest earnings by stealing cars and robbing stores. As a result, Clyde was arrested several more times until, in April 1930, he was eventually sent to Eastham Prison Farm. Eastham had a reputation throughout the state for its dangerous conditions and heavy workloads. It was designed to punish hardened male criminals by making them spend most of their waking hours working in the hot Texas sun.

For Clyde, it wasn't the hot days that were the problem; it was the dark nights when his cellmate would repeatedly rape him. When he could take the abuse no longer, he beat the man to death, thus committing his first murder at the age of 21. By the time he got out of prison the following year, his own sisters barely recognized the hardened criminal their brother had become. His sister Marie later noted, "Something awful sure must have happened to him in prison, because he wasn't the same person when he got out." That was seconded by Ralph Fults, an inmate at Eastham, who said Clyde changed " from a schoolboy to a rattlesnake."

Chapter 3: The Couple

"The road was so dimly lighted

There were no highway signs to guide
But they made up their minds if all roads were blind
They wouldn't give up 'til they died.

The road gets dimmer and dimmer
Sometimes you can hardly see
But it's fight man to man, and do all you can
For they know they can never be free."

In January 1930, Bonnie lost her job at the diner and left her mother's house to stay with a friend in West Dallas who had a broken arm and needed help around the house. One day, while she was in the kitchen making hot chocolate, there was a knock at the door. Her friend called for the person to come in, and Clyde Barrow stepped into the cramped little living room. Coming out of the kitchen to see who was visiting, Bonnie came face to face with the man of her dreams. Though not yet a hardened criminal, Barrow already had a number of crimes under his belt, and he would soon be sent away to Eastham. While he was gone, Bonnie remained faithful to him, building up in her mind a fantasy of the romantic adventures the two of them would enjoy when he got out.

Thus, she ready to join what became known as "The Barrow Gang," which Clyde formed soon after leaving Eastham in February 1932. Armed with an M1919 Browning Automatic Rifle, Clyde was soon out robbing small grocery stores and gas stations. His goal, along with that of his friend Ralph Fults, was to gather enough money and guns to stage a retaliatory raid on Eastham Prison, whom Clyde held responsible for his sexual assaults and other mistreatment. If they could break out other prisoners, all the better.

Bonnie soon earned her place in the group, being captured on April 19 after a failed burglary against a hardware store. She was kept for a few months in Kaufman County jail in Texas until June 17, when the grand jury decided not to indict her because of her youth and previous clean record. Instead, they released her with a stern warning to stay out of trouble in the future. Instead, she quickly returned to Clyde and a life of crime.

However, Ralph Fults, who had been arrested with her, had been convicted and given a much longer sentence. He was never involved with the gang again, but Bonnie and Clyde carried on without him. By this time, Clyde was wanted for the murder of J. N. Bucher, the owner of a store he robbed in Hillsboro, Texas, on April 30, 1932. In actuality, Clyde was probably an accomplice who waited behind the wheel of the getaway car during that robbery, but he would have plenty of blood on his hands soon enough.

Chapter 4: The Barrow Gang

"Now Bonnie and Clyde are the Barrow Gang,
I'm sure you all have read
how they rob and steal and those who squeal
are usually found dying or dead.

There's lots of untruths to these write-ups
They're not so ruthless as that
Their nature is raw, they hate all law
Stool pigeons, spotters, and rats."

In August 1932, Bonnie left the gang long enough to visit her mother in Dallas, and while she was gone, Clyde, along with Raymond Hamilton and Ross Dyer, attended a barn dance just across the Texas state line in Stringtown, Oklahoma. They were sitting outside the dance, drinking, when Stringtown Sheriff C. G. Maxwell and his deputy, Eugene Moore, approached them to find out what they were doing. Though there is no evidence to indicate that either man knew anything about who they were, Barrow still saw a uniform, and that's all it took. He and Hamilton fired on both men, killing Moore. Though Maxwell was seriously injured, he was able to survive the attack and describe the two shooters.

High with a sense of having struck out against authority, Barrow quickly attacked again, this time killing a storekeeper who didn't give up the $28 in his cash register quickly enough. This October 11 robbery, which took place in Sherman, Texas, was yet another example of the escalating violence in the gang's tactics.

On Christmas Eve 1932, 16 year old W. D. Jones became the youngest member of the Barrow gang. A family friend for years, Jones already had a criminal record and naturally looked up to the bad boy Clyde and wanted to be like him. He rode out of Dallas with them that night, and in an interview with Playboy decades later, he described what happened on Christmas Day.

I had got with Clyde and Bonnie the night before in Dallas. Me and L. C., that's Clyde's younger brother, was driving home from a dance in his daddy's old car. Here come Bonnie and Clyde. They honked their car horn and we pulled over. I stayed in the car. L. C. got out and went back to see what they wanted. Then he hollered at me, "Hey, come on back. Clyde wants to talk to you." Clyde was wanted then for murder and kidnaping, but I had knowed him all my life. So I got out and went to his car.

He told me, "We're here to see Momma and Marie." (That's Clyde's baby sister.) "You stay with us while L. C. gets them." I was 16 years old and Clyde was only seven years older, but he always called me "Boy."

Them was Prohibition days and about all there was to drink was home-brew. That's what me and L. C. had been drinking that Christmas Eve and it was about all gone. Clyde had some moonshine in his car, so I stayed with him, like he said, while L. C. fetched his folks. They lived just down the road in back of the filling station Old Man Barrow run.

After the visiting was over, Clyde told me him and Bonnie had been driving a long ways and was tired. He wanted me to go with them so I could keep watch while they got some rest. I went. I know now it was a fool thing to do, but then it seemed sort of big to be out with two famous outlaws. I reckoned Clyde took me along because he had knowed me before and figured he could count on me.

It must have been two o'clock Christmas morning when we checked into a tourist court at Temple. They slept on the bed. I had a pallet on the floor.

Next morning, I changed two tires on that Ford Clyde had. Clyde really banked on them Fords. They was the fastest and the best, and he knew bow to drive them with one foot in the gas tank all the time. We went into town and stopped around the comer from a grocery store.

Clyde handed me an old .41-caliber thumb buster and told me, "Take this, boy, and stand watch while I get us some spending money." Later, I found out that gun wouldn't shoot because there was two broken bullets stuck inside the chamber. I had to punch them out with a stick.

I stood outside the store while Clyde went in. Bonnie was waiting in the car around the corner. After he got the money, we walked away toward Bonnie. Now, the blocks in them days was longer than they are now; and before we got halfway back to the car, Clyde stopped alongside a Model A roadster that had the keys in it. I don't know if he'd seen something over his shoulder that spooked him or what. But he told me, "Get in that car, boy, and start it." I jumped to it. But it was a cold day and the car wouldn't start. Clyde got impatient. He told me to slip over and he'd do it. I scooted over. About then an old man and an old woman run over to the roadster and began yelling, "That's my boy's car! Get out!" Then another woman run up and began making a big fuss. All the time, Clyde was trying to get it started. He told them to stand back and they wouldn't get hurt. Then the guy who owned it run up. Clyde pointed his pistol and yelled, "Get back ' man, or I'll kill you." That man was Doyle Johnson, I learned later. He came on up to the car and reached through the roadster's isinglass window curtains and got Clyde by the throat and tried to choke him.

Clyde hollered, "Stop, man, or I'll kill you." Johnson didn't move, and Clyde done what he had threatened. About then he got the car started and we whipped around the corner to where Bonnie was waiting. We piled into her car and lit a shuck out of town.

It all seemed pointless then as to why Clyde wanted that car. I've thought about it since, and I figure he must have wanted the laws to think we was in Johnson's car. Of course, he didn't have no way of knowing he was gonna have to kill Johnson.

We headed out of town toward Waco. A mile or two down the road, Clyde pulled over and said, "Boy, shinny up that pole and cut them phone wires. We don't want no calls ahead." I done it and we went on.

As I look back, cutting them phone wires was slick. That was about all you had to do to cut off the law in them days. There wasn't no two-way radio hookups like now; and when a police used them long-distance phone wires to call the next town, it run up expenses. Them was hard times and even towns didn't have much to spend. There wasn't as many laws then, either, and they just couldn't catch up with Clyde in them V8 Fords he drove. Ted Hinton and Bob Alcorn, the Dallas lawmen I come to know a year later, told me Clyde was about the best driver in the world. They said them Fords and Clyde's driving was what kept him and Bonnie free them two years. Hell, I knowed that. I rode with him. He had me drive some when he was tired, but Clyde stayed behind the' wheel when the heat was close. He believed in a nonstop jump in territory -- sometimes as much as 1000 miles --whenever it got hot behind. He and Bonnie didn't in- tend to ever be taken alive. They was hell-bent on running till the end, and they knowed there was only one end for them. Sometimes I thought Clyde liked the running. He dreaded getting caught, but he never give up robbing to work for a living. I reckon Clyde just didn't want to work like other folks. For one thing, he never liked getting his hands dirty.

27 year old Doyle Johnson was a new father who was on his way home for Christmas dinner. Though Jones claimed Clyde shot Johnson, accounts of the shooting claimed the firing came from the passenger side, implicating Jones. According to Jones, those accounts gave Clyde all he needed to ensure Jones had to stay with the gang, and Clyde told the youngster, "Boy, you can't go home. You got murder on you, just like me."

Regardless of who pulled the trigger, the pair stole Johnson's car and drove it to Tarrant County, where, two weeks later, they killed Deputy Sheriff Malcolm Davis. Like Doyle Johnson, Davis was in the wrong place at the wrong time. He had been staking out a quiet part of town waiting for another wanted criminal when Clyde and Jones came upon the scene accidentally. The murder of Deputy Sheriff Davis was Clyde's 5th killing since his February 1932 release, and he had been involved in the grave wounding of another officer as well.

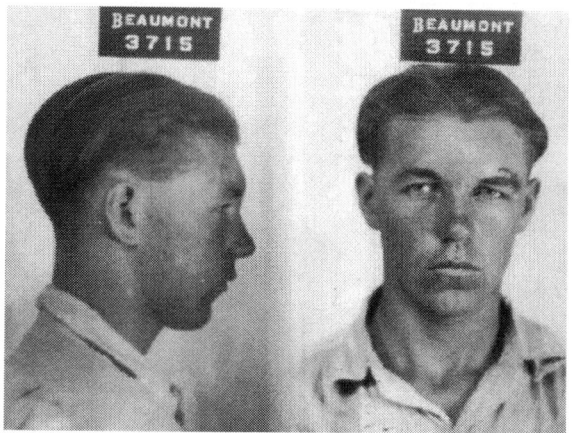

1931 mugshot of 15 year old William Daniel Jones. Jones and his friend L.C. Barrow were arrested after stealing and crashing a car.

In late March 1933, Clyde's brother Buck was finally released from prison after having been given a full pardon by the governor of Texas. He and his wife, Blanche, moved in with Bonnie, Clyde and Jones at 3347 ½ Oakridge Drive in Joplin, Missouri. They lived a quiet life and might well indeed have escaped notice and arrest but for the group's insistence on regularly hosting noisy card games that went until all hours of the night and were fueled by the newly legalized beer available with the end of Prohibition. The group routinely went through as much as a case of beer each evening, and during one particularly rowdy party, Clyde accidentally shot off his rifle, causing the neighbors to complain to the local police force.

Buck and Blanche Barrow

Believing that they were only dealing with a bunch of rowdy citizens, five police officers surrounded the garage apartment on April 13, 1933, but when they called for those inside to come out with their hands up, everyone except Blanch came out shooting. They killed Detective McGinnis on the spot, while Constable Harryman later died of his wounds. Then, with Bonnie providing cover fire, the men jumped in the car and got it started. They swung by to grab Bonnie and then headed down the street after Blanche, who had gone after Snow Ball, her little white dog.

The Joplin hideout

When the dust settled, one officer had a face full of splinters from wood thrown at him by Bonnie's shooting, one officer was dead, another was dying and two had escaped uninjured. Of the gang, young Jones was the most seriously injured, having been shot in the side. Buck was bleeding from where a ricocheted bullet grazed him and Clyde had a bullet hole in his suitcase.

What the group left behind proved to be much more important to the legend than anything they took with them. The police found confirming evidence of all involved, including Buck and Blanche Barrow's marriage licens,e as well as his three week old parole papers. They also found a significant collection of guns and a camera with several rolls of undeveloped film. Most interesting of all, they found the poem "Suicide Sal," which had been written by Bonnie.

16 year old W.D. Jones posing

Because they had no photo lab of their own, the police took the film to the local paper, *The Joplin Globe*, for development. As a result, a full page story soon ran featuring a cigar smoking Bonnie holding a pistol, Clyde and Buck playing around while pointing guns at each other, a host of other salacious pictures of the two couples, and Bonnie's poem "Suicide Sal." The newly formed newswire service picked up the story, and "The Barrow Gang" became front page news all over the country. Jones explained the origins of the photos that made the gang famous:

> Bonnie smoked cigarettes, but that cigar bit folks like to tell about is phony. I guess I got that started when. I gave her my cigar to hold when I was making her picture. I made most of them pictures the laws picked up when we fled Joplin, Missouri, leaving

everything in the apartment except the guns. I seen a lot of them pictures in the newspapers afterward -- Them little poems Bonnie made up made the papers, too. She would think up rhymes in her head and put them down on paper when we stopped. Some of them she kept, but she threw a lot of them away.

Chapter 5: Celebrities

Bonnie and Clyde were probably certain of their ultimate fate, but they almost certainly relished their fame and publicity at the same time. In April 1934, Henry Ford received a letter purportedly authored by Clyde thanking the famous car maker for producing Clyde's favorite kind of car:

Mr. Henry Ford

Detroit Mich.

Dear Sir: --

While I still have got breath in my lungs I will tell you what a dandy car you make. I have drove Fords exclusively when I could get away with one. For sustained speed and freedom from trouble the Ford has got ever other car skinned and even if my business hasen't been strickly legal it don't hurt anything to tell you what a fine car you got in the V8 --

Yours truly

Clyde Champion Barrow

While it's still unclear whether Clyde actually wrote that letter, historians and analysts believe that the spelling errors can be explained by his lack of education, and there's no doubt Clyde was a big fan of the V-8. Others believe that the handwriting of the letter resemble Bonnie's handwriting. Of course, if Clyde didn't author it, the letter was a clear example of Clyde's notoriety, and a short time afterward Ford received a letter purported to be from John Dillinger (though the Dillinger letter was later proven to be a fraud).

However, the publicity came at a cost. With the published photos plastering their faces on newspapers across the nation, it became more and more dangerous for anyone from the gang to appear in public. For that reason, the gang was constantly on the move, and over the next three months they worked their way from Texas to Minnesota, stopping along the way in Lucerne, Indiana in May to try to rob a bank. Though they failed in that job, they succeeded a little while later in Okabena, Minnesota. As a result of their frequent travels, the Barrow Gang got credit for crimes they didn't actually commit, while false sightings in places they were far away from also became common. Jones recounted one example:

> Some of the tales about us robbing banks all the time ain't true, either. The time I was with Clyde and Bonnie, we never made a bank job. He liked grocery stores, filling stations and places there was a payroll. Why should we rob a bank? There was never much money in the banks back in them days in the Southwest. But that's not the way the papers put it. They'd write we was heisting a bank in Texas when we was actually off in Tennessee or somewhere else. I remember one time we stopped at a tourist court in a little town. I went across the road to an inn to get some sandwiches. The waiter was all excited. "Bonnie and Clyde was just here," he told me. "They stopped for gas. The police come out, but they got here too late. Bonnie and Clyde was already gone and they couldn't catch them." It shook me some when he said that, but I stayed calm.
>
> I took the food back to the tourist cabin and told Clyde what the man had said. He got a good laugh out of that, but after we had eat, he said, "You know, that man might have been giving us a tip. He might have recognized us. We better move on."

Eventually, Henry Methvin had joined the gang, and Methvin would prove to be the "weak link" in the chain that would eventually break.

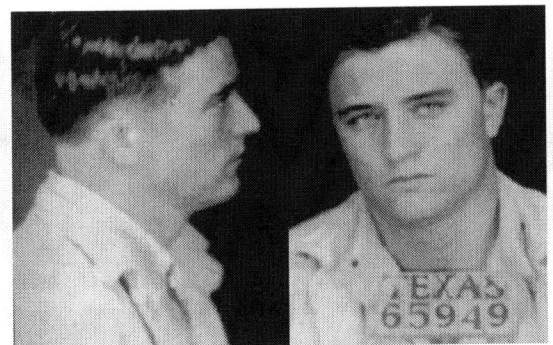

```
HENRY METHVIN.
Age 20 (1931).Ht 5-9½ Wt 170. Hair Lt.Brown
Eyes blue. Complex Fair. Marks and Scars.
1 dim horizontal cut scar left middle
finger 1st joint 2 dagger pierced and
lettered "love" right forearm inner.
```

Methvin's mugshot

While the American public was fascinated by the notion of young lovers on the run, the Barrow Gang faced a much starker reality. Because they now lived in constant fear of being recognized, the Barrow Gang no longer ate in restaurants or slept in motels. Instead, they camped in the woods outside of towns, cooked their meals over make shift fires and bathed in cold, shallow streams. On top of all that, the gang constantly had to steal new cars. As Jones later explained:

> Clyde drove most always, 'cause he didn't trust nobody else to drive like he could. As for me working on the car, I'd change a tire or a battery or something like that. But we'd junk a car if anything went wrong with it and get another one. I don't know how many cars I stole for Clyde. I do remember we never kept one more than a week or so, because it'd get too hot…

> We never stayed long in one place. It was too risky. We had to keep moving. When our clothes got dirty, we'd take them to a cleaners if we thought it was safe. But we didn't wait until they was ready. We'd drive on somewhere else and, in a week or two, swing back to pick them up, if there was no heat behind. Sometimes we never got back. We'd buy new clothes.

> Any shopping we done was done alone. Me and Clyde would wait in the car down the street while Bonnie went in and got what she wanted. Or he would go in a store while we waited out in the car.

I always figured some of them reporters was holed up somewhere with some booze during the time they claimed they'd been off with the law in hot pursuit of the outrageous Barrow gang. They was just writing from their imagination, it seemed to me. I couldn't read what they was saying in the papers then, but we'd pick up the newspaper in whatever little town we was traveling through and Bonnie would read it aloud. That way, we kept up with where the law thought we was and we'd head in the opposite direction.

These conditions, along with the fact that the five members spent most of their days riding around in cars lacking air conditioning, made life very unpleasant for everyone. Jones noted that the passengers often rode for hours in complete silence:

There was never a whole lot of talk among us when we was on the road. Often what seemed like hours of silence would be broken as Clyde looked at her and said something like, "Honey, _ as soon as I find a place, I'm gonna stop. I'm tired and want to get some rest." He always called her "Honey" or "Baby" and she called him "Daddy" or "Honey." They called me "Boy." I got to where I called Bonnie "Sis" and Clyde "Bud." We couldn't say each other's names, because somebody at a filling station or a tourist court might pick up on them and call, the 'law.

Bonnie was always agreeable with Clyde, but they did have some fallings out. I've seen them fall out over a can of sardines. He jerked it out of her hands and opened it with his pocketknife, and her trying to tell him it had an opener. But I never heard them call each other bad names. They hardly ever used dirty words. I've heard today's teenagers use words worse than Clyde and Bonnie, and they was deadly outlaws.

Sometimes, when she got puffed up about something, Clyde would kid her and say, "Why don't you go on home to Momma, baby? You probably wouldn't get more than ninety-nine years. Texas hasn't sent a woman to the chair yet, and I'd send in my recommendation for leniency." She'd laugh at him then and everything would be smooth again.

Jones ultimately reached the point that he couldn't stand the confinement anymore and stole a car to get away from everyone. However, the loneliness soon changed his mind, and he returned to the gang on June 8, 1933.

Two days later, perhaps while drinking, arguing or both, Clyde flipped the car that he, Bonnie and Jones were riding in. While he and Jones walked away unscathed, Bonnie's leg was very badly burned. The two men managed to get Bonnie to a nearby farm, where a Mrs. Pritchard examined the leg, saw that it was burned to the bone near the knee and insisted that they needed to call a doctor. When Clyde seemed reluctant, Mr. Pritchard became suspicious and slipped away to call the police. Upon noticing his host was missing, Clyde picked up the crying Bonnie and, with Jones on his heels, ran out the door, jumping in Pritchard's car and driving away.

From there they drove to Fort Smith, Arkansas, where they got a room in a tourist court. Clyde finally agreed to bring in a doctor, who insisted that Bonnie needed round the clock nursing. Unable to risk taking her to a hospital, he hired a private nurse to care for her. He also contacted Bonnie's sister, Billie Jean, who travelled from Texas to help care for her sister.

In need of quick money, Buck Barrow and Jones attempted and failed to rob a local bank in Alma, Arkansas, killing Marshal Henry Humphrey in the process. This brought out every lawman in the area, and forced the group to go on the run again, dragging the nearly delirious Bonnie with them. According to Jones, "Bonnie never got over that burn. Even after it healed over, her leg was drawn under her. She had to just hop or hobble along. When she was so bad at first, we had to carry her to the toilet and take her off when she finished and put her back in bed.

Chapter 6: The Manhunt

"If a policeman is killed in Dallas
And they have no clue or guide
If they can't find a fiend, just wipe the slate clean
And hang it on Bonnie and Clyde.

There's two crimes committed in America
Not accredited to the Barrow Mob
They had no hand in the kidnap demand
Nor the Kansas City Depot job."

The Red Crown Tourist Court

The gang's next stop was the Red Crown Tourist Court in Platte City, Missouri, where they rented both the small brick cabins available on July 19, 1933. Unbeknownst to them, the tavern by the same name, located just across the street, was a favorite hang-out for Missouri Highway Patrolmen. Still, had they behaved themselves, they might have avoided notice, but just like in Joplin, the Barrow Gang proved incapable of avoiding notice.

Blanche made the first mistake by strolling into the tourist court office wearing riding breeches and registering only three people. The owner of the tourist court, Neal Houser, knew that the average woman driving with her family through Missouri did not wear riding breeches. On top of that, when he looked out the window, he saw clearly that more than three people were getting out of the car, including what appeared to be crippled women being carried. Furthermore, Houser also also noticed that they backed their car into the driveway, as if ready to make a quick getaway. The gang also paid for both their lodging and five meals each day with coins instead of bills, and with all that Houser was thoroughly suspicious. However, the icing on the cake was that they covered all the windows, which were already curtained, with sheets of newspaper. Houser decided to stroll across the street and mention his unusual guests to one of the Highway Patrolmen, Captain William Baxter, who was drinking coffee at the tavern.

In the meantime, local Sheriff Holt Coffey received word that the infamous Bonnie had been injured and that the gang was on the run again. So when the local druggist called and told him about some suspicious looking characters who had come by to purchase bandages and atropine sulfate (used for treating burns), he decided to put a man near the tourist court to see what was going on. He also contacted Baxter, who agreed that this might be the real deal. Together they planned a raid, sending to nearby Kansas City for reinforcements and an armored car.

The same night the gang arrived, at 11:00 p.m., Coffey, Baxter and their men surrounded the cabins, sending an officer to bang on the door and order everyone out. Instead, all three men began firing out the doors and windows. Much to the gang's surprise, the "local yokels" they expected returned fire with submachine guns, forcing them to take cover on the floor. Buck, refusing to take cover, attempted to fire back and was hit in the head by two rounds.

Clyde carried the unconscious Bonnie to the garage and threw her in the back seat of the car while Jones checked outside for an escape route. Clyde went back and grabbed Buck while Jones fired on the armored car blocking them in. The driver pulled out of the line of fire, allowing the gang to shoot its way out and escape. During the chaos, Jones had been shot in the shoulder, and Blanche had been blinded by shards of glass that struck her in both eyes.

With four moaning, injured people in the car, Clyde drove through the dark night. Five days later they made camp in a disused amusement park in Dexter, Iowa, but their presence was soon noted by local citizens, who alerted the police. This time, the police called on every man in the community who could fire a gun to help surround the five and open fire. While Bonnie, Clyde and Jones were able to escape, they left the dying Buck behind, along with Blanche. Buck died a few days later, and Blanche was later convicted as an accessory to murder and served ten years in prison.

The arrest of Blanche Barrow

Still determined to live long enough to complete his revenge, Clyde dragged the injured Bonnie and W.D. northwest to Colorado, then back to Minnesota and then south again to Mississippi, pulling mostly small jobs so that they had spending money. One notable exception was when the three robbed the armory in Plattville, Illinois, taking with them three new Browning Automatic Rifles, a number of handguns and as much ammunition as they could carry.

After six weeks on the run, the trio returned to Dallas in September to visit their families. It seems that by now Bonnie and Clyde knew that the end was near, and in a way the trip seemed like one last chance to come home to say good bye. By now, Jones had had enough, and he left with their permission to visit his mother and not return:

I left Clyde and Bonnie after they was healed up enough to get by without me. Clyde put me out to steal a car and I hooked 'em back to Texas.

I'd had enough blood and hell.

But it wasn't done yet. I had to pay. A boy in Houston, where I was working for a vegetable peddler, knowed me and turned me in to the law. They tried me for killing a sheriff's man at Dallas. Clyde done it, but I was glad to take the rap. Arkansas wanted to extradite me, and. I sure didn't want to go to no Arkansas prison. I figure now that if Arkansas had got me, one of them skeletons they've dug up there might have been me.

As Jones indicated, he was quickly arrested in Houston, on November 16. He would hear about the final demise of Bonnie and Clyde from a jail cell.

Leaving Bonnie with her family, Clyde went about the Texas countryside, executing small time robberies with the help of local hoodlums who were excited to get to pull a job with the notorious Clyde Barrow. On November 22, he took Bonnie with him to Sowers, Texas to visit some more family members, but Dallas Sheriff Smoot Schmid got wind of their plans and ambushed the two, firing on their car. While they got away, they were both shot in the legs by a single bullet from a BAR. A few days later, a Dallas grand jury would finally indict Bonnie for the murder of Deputy Malcolm Davis. Though Bonnie was often portrayed in the media as the mastermind and the cold-blooded killer in the group, Jones claimed that it was quite the opposite: "Bonnie was the only one Clyde trusted all the way. But not even Bonnie had a voice in the decisions. His leadership was undisputed. She always agreed with him when he ' hinted he might like to hear her advice on something. As far as I know, Bonnie never packed a gun. Maybe she'd help carry what we had in the car into a tourist-court room. But during the five big gun battles I was with them, she never fired a gun. But I'll say she was a hell of a loader."

The two spent the month of December laying low, perhaps hoping to spend what they might have sensed would be their last Christmas quietly. However, they started 1934 off with a bang, both literally and figuratively, when Clyde finally attacked the Eastham State Prison. On January 16 he sprung his friends Raymond Hamilton and Henry Methvin from the hell-hole that had been the source of so much of his pain. In the process, he killed a prison officer, Major Joe Crowson.

There is a reason for the old saying "don't mess with Texas" and Clyde's attack on the prison brought the force of the entire Lone Star State down on his head, in addition to all the federal officials who were already looking for him. The Texas Department of Corrections brought one of the most famous Texas Rangers in history, Captain Frank A. Hamer, out of retirement to go after what was left of the Barrow Gang. Hamer was the perfect man for the job, unafraid to kill anyone that might harm a fellow Texan. According to his record, he had personally sent more than 50 criminals to their graves and had been wounded 17 times in the process. Unlike some others in the organization, he made it clear that he would have no problem firing on Bonnie Parker, even though she was a woman.

Beginning on February 10, 1934, Hamer had one purpose: capture Bonnie and Clyde, dead or alive.

Hamer

Chapter 7: Public Reaction

>From heartbreak some people have suffered
>From weariness some people have died
>But all in all, our troubles are small
>'Til we get like Bonnie and Clyde.
>
>A newsboy once said to his buddy
>"I wish old Clyde would get jumped
>In these hard times we's get a few dimes
>If five or six cops would get bumped."

In many ways it's impossible today for cold-blooded cop killers to become folk heroes, but there were several extenuating circumstances about Depression Era America that made it possible. First, when Bonnie and Clyde first came on the scene in 1932, the American people were still smarting from what they perceived to be a betrayal of their hopes and dreams. The fathers of middle class families had lived through a World War with the promise that, once the Kaiser was beat, all would be well. They had returned home to hope for a secure future based on hard work and careful saving. The Financial Crash of 1929 had smashed their hopes to pieces and left most of them even poorer than when they had started. In the secret places that they would not admit, perhaps not even to themselves, Clyde's reign of terror against the established systems seemed a little like sweet revenge.

On the other hand, Bonnie's devil may care attitude had a certain attraction for the hardworking housewife. Like Bonnie, they had once been free to stay up late and bob their hair. They had traded that for the promise of romantic and financial security. Many a 30 year old woman with four or five children to feed had only just a few years earlier been a prosperous bride with the world at her feet. She and her husband had anticipated only continued prosperity, thanks to a booming economy and cheap land. Then the bank foreclosed and they traded their little house with a picket fence for a shack in the Dust Bowl or a one room walk-up on the backside of a tenement. For some of these women, when Bonnie took a shot at one man who stood between her and what she wanted, she was taking a shot at all the men who had ever let some woman down.

Then, of course, there was the way the papers of the day spun the stories. While reporters did mention the murders, they also told fascinating tales of victims kidnapped by the gang only to be turned loose a few hours or days later with money to get home with. Some of these victims even spoke well of their captors, referring to their good looks or polite manners.

However, any good opinion the public had quickly evaporated on April 1, 1934. That day, Easter Sunday, the gang killed two highway patrolmen, H.D. Murphy and Edward Wheeler, in Grapevine, Texas. Though Methvin fired the first shot, and he later claimed Bonnie walked up to the officer with the intention of helping, rumors flew around the country that she had not only fired on the officers, but that she had stood laughing over the dead officer's body. Others claimed that she left behind a cigar butt with her own teeth marks on it. By the time it was later reported that Bonnie had nothing to do with this shooting, and may have even been passed out pain killers, their public reputation was tarnished.

There was something about this attack that seemed worse to the public. Maybe it was that it happened on what, to most of the country, was one of the most sacred days of the year. Maybe it was because Murphy's young bride-to-be attended his funeral in her wedding gown. Whatever the reason, the public was now thoroughly incensed at the lawlessness around them and wanted it stopped. The Highway Patrol and the governor's office offered a combined reward of $2,000 for the bodies of gang, but specifically for Bonnie and Clyde.

Either unaware of or unconcerned about their new level of notoriety, Clyde and Methvin gunned down 60 year old Constable Cal Campbell five days later just outside of Commerce, Oklahoma. On the same day, they kidnapped the town police chief, Percy Boyd, and then turned him loose with a clean shirt and money to get home with. According to Boyd, Bonnie asked that he tell the world she did not smoke cigars. It seems that of all the things that paper was accusing her of, that was the one that bothered her most.

With Boyd's eyewitness testimony to Campbell's murder, the Oklahoma authorities were able to issue warrants for the arrest of Clyde Barrow and Bonnie Parker specifically. On the other hand, they merely referred to Methvin as "John Doe." This marked the first time that Bonnie was actually seen shooting someone.

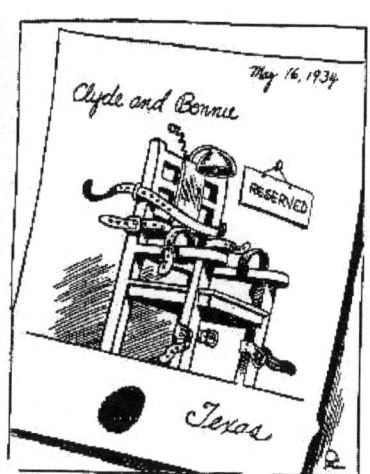

Chapter 8: The Inevitable

> "They don't think they're tough or desperate
> They know the law always wins
> They've been shot at before, but they do not ignore
> That death is the wages of sin.
>
> Some day they'll go down together
> And they'll bury them side by side
> To few it'll be grief, to the law a relief
> But it's death for Bonnie and Clyde."

Beginning with his appointment to the case on February 10, Frank Hamer stalked every move that the remaining Barrow Gang made. One of the things he discovered was that they tended to move in a circular pattern along the states lines of Texas, Louisiana, Arkansas, Oklahoma and Kansas. By moving along state lines, they were able to avoid capture by local officers or highway patrolmen who could not cross state lines. Another thing that he noticed was that the gang tended to visit their families at regular intervals. According to his calculations, the next family due for a visit was Methvin's family in Louisiana.

Because he had a set pattern of behavior, Hamer was able to anticipate his next move and plan accordingly. In mid-May, 1934, Hamer requisitioned a large number of Browning Automatic Rifles and 20 rounds of armor piercing bullets. Then, on May 21, he left Texas with four hand-picked posse members and traveled to Shreveport, Louisiana. There they waited until word reached them through their sources that the trio were heading to Bienville Parish. The three gang members agreed that, in case they became separated, they would meet on an abandoned stretch of highway near Methvin's parents' home. Methvin's father became aware of this arrangement and, under increased pressure from the police, exchanged the information for a promise that his son would not receive the death penalty if captured.

The posse: standing: Ted Hinton, Prentiss Oakley, Manny Gault; seated: Bob Alcorn, Henderson Jordan and Hamer.

Hamer had chosen his posse well. In addition to himself, there was Ted Hinton, who knew Bonnie from her waitressing days, as well as Bob Alcorn, who knew Clyde on sight. There was also former Ranger Manny Gaul, Sheriff Henderson Jordan from Bienville, and his deputy, Prentiss Oakley. Together the men waited outside the rendezvous point on Highway 154 for the little group to show up.

At about 9:00 on the morning of May 23, 1934, the waiting posse heard a car fast approaching. Looking through the bushes they quickly identified it as the stolen Ford that Clyde had last been seen driving. It pulled up alongside Ivan Methvin's truck, placed there by Hamer to attract Clyde's attention and to place his car in the best position for the ambush. The five officers opened fire, spraying the Ford and its occupants with approximately 130 rounds of ammunition. According to interviews with Alcorn and Hinton:

It was about 9 a. m., when we finally sighted the car. It was a gray V-8 coach, and that was the car we were looking for. We had been waiting at the top of a steep hill, and the car had to slow down as it neared the top. There wasn't any time to think. We didn't have a minute to wonder if we were coming out alive. The name Clyde Barrow and all the terror and danger it involved didn't mean a thing. There were two people in that car and they probably were Clyde and Bonnie. And that car was getting nearer.

There must have been a signal given, but "who it came from is another thing. We just all acted together, stepped out into the road and raised our guns. We all yelled "Halt!" at once.

They didn't halt. The car was going slowly and Clyde let go of the wheel. We could see him grab at a gun in his lap. Bonnie was going for something on the other side.

Then all hell broke loose. There were six men shooting at once. Machine guns? No, thank God. We had shotguns and Browning automatics. We had tried machine guns once before....

You couldn't hear any one shot. It was just a roar, a continuous roar, and it kept up for several minutes. We emptied our guns, reloaded and kept shooting. No chances with Clyde and Bonnie.

As we jumped into sight, I could see Clyde reaching as if to get his gun. But he never had a chance to fire a shot. Neither did Bonnie, though we learned a few minutes later that they both were carrying rifles across their laps.

Each of us six officers had a shotgun and an automatic rifle and pistols.

We opened fire with the automatic rifles. They were emptied before the car got even with us. Then we used shotguns.

After shooting the shotguns, we emptied the pistols at the car, which had passed us and ran into a ditch about 50 yards on down the road. It almost turned over. We kept shooting at the car even after it stopped. We weren't taking any chances.

There was smoke coming from the car, and it looked like it was on fire. I guess this was caused when one of the shotguns Clyde or Bonnie had across their laps went off. They did not have time to raise their guns, but the tightening of their muscles as they were filled with lead might have pressed the trigger. The blast at close range almost tore off ...the door.

We all ran up to the car. Ted opened the door on Bonnie's side and she almost fell out.

She was sitting with her head down between her knees, bent over the gun that was in her lap. Her right hand had been shot away. She was also shot in the mouth, and I learned later that there were about 40 other bullet holes in her.

The door on Clyde's side would not open. His head was hanging out the window.

He too had a shotgun across his lap and a pistol in his hand. The back of his head was shot off.

Bob knew right away that we had at last got the right ones. He knew Clyde when the punk was stealing automobiles. He also knew Bonnie, who used to be a waitress near the courthouse. You can imagine how we felt. Our first thought was to tell the boss, Sheriff Smoot Schmid so we got to the nearest town as quickly as we could and telephoned.

"Did you sleep good last night?" Ted asked Smoot. "No, I didn't." he answered. "Well, you can go on home and sleep now." Ted told him. "We just killed em both." Smoot dropped the phone. Oakley meanwhile went back to Arcadia for the coroner. In the back of the car we found three machine rifles, two automatic shotguns, 10 automatic pistols and 1500 rounds of ammunition. There were a couple of magazines, a detective and a love story. In the seat beside Clyde and Bonnie was a bacon and lettuce sandwich.

Before we got back to the car, however, people just sprang up from everywhere.

Without removing the bodies, we hitched the car onto the back of a truck and towed it into Arcadia, where the bodies were taken to the undertakers. That little town was filled with cars and people.

Among the people who "sprang from everywhere" were women who tried to cut of locks of Bonnie's hair and pieces of her dress. Another man tried to cut off Clyde's trigger finger while another went after his left ear. According to the official coroner's report, Clyde was shot 17 times and Bonnie 26. Each had several headshots, any one of which would have killed them instantly. The undertaker reported having difficulty embalming the body because they were too full of holes to hold the embalming fluid.

Among the 12,000 people that rushed into the little town in the hopes of seeing a piece of history was one lone farmer with a sad, weather beaten face. Henry Barrow had been called in by the police to make an official identification of what was left of his son's body. Afterwards he sat alone in the back of the furniture store where the bodies had been taken and wept. There was also a young man in his mid-20s, dress in a quiet suit. He was Buster Parker, and he was there to bring his sister's body home.

Another person called in that day to help confirm the identities of the dead was H. D. Darby. The previous year, Bonnie and Clyde had stolen his car and kidnapped him and his girlfriend. Giddy and talkative with excitement, Bonnie had asked him what he did for a living. When he replied that he was an undertaker, she cackled with laughter and observed that perhaps one day he'd get to work on her. In fact he did, assisting Mr. McClure of McClure's Funeral Parlor with preparing her body for burial.

Like their short lives, Bonnie and Clyde's respective funerals got completely out of hand. Bonnie's funeral, held at the McCamy-Campbell Funeral Home in Dallas, was inundated with flowers, including arrangements that allegedly came from other "public enemies" such as John Dillinger and Pretty Boy Floyd. However, no bouquet was a large as the one from a group of Dallas news boys, who paid tribute to the woman whose death had allowed them to sell more than half a million papers in one day. 20,000 people showed up at the Fishtrap Cemetery for her burial, making it nearly impossible for the family to get to the gravesite.

Clyde's funeral was private and held at the chapel of the Sparkman-Holtz-Brand Funeral Home in Dallas. He was buried in the Western Heights Cemetery, next to his brother, Buck. A single head stone marks both their graves and says, simply, "gone but not forgotten," just as Clyde had earlier requested.

While this epitaph could not be more appropriate (no one who hears his story will ever forget Clyde Barrow,) it also could not be more poignant. As a young man, he was the fifth of a large, very poor family where there appears to have never been enough of anything, including attention, to go around. Desperate for adventure and money, he made the poor choice of breaking the law. However, the law in turn broke him. The cruelty of the Texas penitentiary system at that time turned a wayward boy into a hardened criminal, and the crimes perpetrated against him while he was in custody played a role in creating Clyde the murderer.

And what of Bonnie? What made a good student turn into a bad moll? For her, it seems that she never overcame the loss of her father at such an age. Good grades may have been her way of gaining family approval and affection until peer acceptance became more important. Then her bad marriage, built on the hope of finally having a man to count on soured her to the possibility of ever being a fully functioning adult and drove her instead toward a life of doing whatever felt good at the moment. She attached herself fully to Clyde, and when it became clear that he would likely die in a hail of bullets, she determined she wanted nothing less than that for herself. In the end, they both got what they wanted.

Chapter 9: The Legend of Bonnie and Clyde

To an extent, the deaths of Bonnie and Clyde signaled the apex of the "Public Enemies Era", and in the next few months, Dillinger, Baby Face Nelson and Pretty Boy Floyd would all be shot dead as well. To help prevent more public enemies, the federal government stepped up their efforts by making bank robbery and kidnapping federal offenses, thus allowing the FBI to get involved in those kinds of crimes.

By then, of course, Bonnie and Clyde had become legends, and their romance, whirlwind lives and ultimate fates made their story a natural on the silver screen. Within decades, Hollywood had depicted their story several times, books had been written, and musicians wrote songs referencing them. In 1967, Warren Beatty and Faye Dunaway added their starpower and striking good looks to the outlaws.

While their story is certainly worth telling, though perhaps not in the sensationalized, romantic way the criminals are often depicted, the portrayals of Bonnie and Clyde are (not surprisingly) often at odds with reality. Far from being swashbuckling, W.D. Jones described Clyde as a young, serious man with a small build:

"I was in the joint when word came on May 23, 1934, that Clyde and Bonnie was killed near Arcadia, Louisiana. I've heard stories since that Clyde was homosexual, or, as they say in the pen, a 'punk,' but they ain't true. Maybe it was Clyde's quiet, polite manner and his slight build that fooled folks.

He was only about five feet, six inches tall and he weighed no more than 135 pounds. Me and him was about the same size, and we used to wear each other's clothes. Clyde had dark hair that was wavy. He never had a beard. Even when he didn't shave, all he had on his chin was fuzz.

Another way that story might have got started was his wearing a wig sometimes when him and Bonnie had to drive through a town where they might be recognized. He wore the wig for disguise and for no other reason.

Clyde never walked right, either. He'd chopped off his big toe and part of the second toe on his left foot when he was in prison, because he couldn't keep up, with the pace the farm boss set.

Or the story could have come from sensation writers who believed anything dropped on them and who blew it to proportions that suited their imagination."

Jones also described Clyde as both polite and even not above praying:

Clyde had good manners, just naturally. It fooled lots of folks, like that policeman in Missouri. We was driving over a bridge and the motor law rolled up beside us and told us to pull over, Clyde smiled and told him, "Just a minute, sir."

It was night and Clyde wanted to get off that bridge before he stopped. But that policeman come on real nasty. "Stop right here now," he said.

Clyde kept right on going and saying, "Just a minute, sir." When we got off the bridge, Clyde turned up a little street and stopped. The policeman come up to the door. That's when Clyde throwed that little shotgun in his face, and that law done a turn around.

Clyde liked to stay sharp and would sometimes hit the car brakes of a sudden, bounce out to the roadside and open up with that cutoff automatic rifle on a tree or a sign for practice. He was never more than an arm's reach from a gun, even in bed, or out of bed on the floor in the night, when he thought we was all asleep and couldn't see him kneeling there. I seen it more than once. He prayed. I reckon he was praying for his soul. Maybe it was for more life. He knowed it would end soon, but he didn't intend for it to be in jail."

Fittingly, it was Jones who dispelled much of the myth-making surrounding the two in his interview with Playboy shortly after the popular 1967 movie about Bonnie and Clyde. "That Bonnie and Clyde movie made it all look sort of glamorous, but like I told them teenaged boys sitting near me at the drive-in showing: 'Take it from an old man who was there. It was hell.'"

Clyde and Jones

The Trail's End

You've read the story of Jesse James
of how he lived and died.
If you're still in need;
of something to read,
here's the story of Bonnie and Clyde.

Now Bonnie and Clyde are the Barrow gang
I'm sure you all have read.
how they rob and steal;
and those who squeal,
are usually found dying or dead.

There's lots of untruths to these write-ups;
they're not as ruthless as that.
their nature is raw;
they hate all the law,
the stool pidgeons, spotters and rats.

They call them cold-blooded killers
they say they are heartless and mean.
But I say this with pride
that I once knew Clyde,
when he was honest and upright and clean.

But the law fooled around;
kept taking him down,
and locking him up in a cell.
Till he said to me;
"I'll never be free,
so I'll meet a few of them in hell"

The road was so dimly lighted
there were no highway signs to guide.
But they made up their minds;
if all roads were blind,
they wouldn't give up till they died.

The road gets dimmer and dimmer
sometimes you can hardly see.
But it's fight man to man
and do all you can,
for they know they can never be free.

From heart-break some people have suffered
from weariness some people have died.
But take it all in all;
our troubles are small,
till we get like Bonnie and Clyde.

If a policeman is killed in Dallas
and they have no clue or guide.
If they can't find a fiend,
they just wipe their slate clean
and hang it on Bonnie and Clyde.

There's two crimes committed in America
not accredited to the Barrow mob.
They had no hand;
in the kidnap demand,
nor the Kansas City Depot job.

A newsboy once said to his buddy;
"I wish old Clyde would get jumped.
In these awfull hard times;
we'd make a few dimes,
if five or six cops would get bumped"

The police haven't got the report yet
but Clyde called me up today.
He said,"Don't start any fights;
we aren't working nights,
we're joining the NRA."

From Irving to West Dallas viaduct
is known as the Great Divide.
Where the women are kin;
and the men are men,
and they won't "stool" on Bonnie and Clyde.

If they try to act like citizens
and rent them a nice little flat.
About the third night;
they're invited to fight,
by a sub-gun's rat-tat-tat.

They don't think they're too smart or desperate
they know that the law always wins.
They've been shot at before;

but they do not ignore,
that death is the wages of sin.

Some day they'll go down together
they'll bury them side by side.
To few it'll be grief,
to the law a relief
but it's death for Bonnie and Clyde.

Suicide Sal

We each of us have a good "alibi"
For being down here in the "joint"
But few of them really are justified
If you get right down to the point.

You've heard of a woman's glory
Being spent on a "downright cur"
Still you can't always judge the story
As true, being told by her.

As long as I've stayed on this "island"
And heard "confidence tales" from each "gal"
Only one seemed interesting and truthful-
The story of "Suicide Sal".

Now "Sal" was a gal of rare beauty,
Though her features were coarse and tough;
She never once faltered from duty
To play on the "up and up".

"Sal" told me this tale on the evening
Before she was turned out "free"
And I'll do my best to relate it
Just as she told it to me:

I was born on a ranch in Wyoming;
Not treated like Helen of Troy,
I was taught that "rods were rulers"
And "ranked" as a greasy cowboy.

Then I left my old home for the city

To play in its mad dizzy whirl,
Not knowing how little of pity
It holds for a country girl.

There I fell for "the line" of a "henchman"
A "professional killer" from "Chi"
I couldn't help loving him madly,
For him even I would die.

One year we were desperately happy
Our "ill gotten gains" we spent free,
I was taught the ways of the "underworld"
Jack was just like a "god" to me.

I got on the "F.B.A." payroll
To get the "inside lay" of the "job"
The bank was "turning big money"!
It looked like a "cinch for the mob".

Eighty grand without even a "rumble"-
Jack was last with the "loot" in the door,
When the "teller" dead-aimed a revolver
From where they forced him to lie on the floor.

I knew I had only a moment-
He would surely get Jack as he ran,
So I "staged" a "big fade out" beside him
And knocked the forty-five out of his hand.

They "rapped me down big" at the station,
And informed me that I'd get the blame
For the "dramatic stunt" pulled on the "teller"
Looked to them, too much like a "game".

The "police" called it a "frame-up"
Said it was an "inside job"
But I steadily denied any knowledge
Or dealings with "underworld mobs".

The "gang" hired a couple of lawyers,

The best "fixers" in any mans town,
But it takes more than lawyers and money
When Uncle Sam starts "shaking you down".

I was charged as a "scion of gangland"
And tried for my wages of sin,
The "dirty dozen" found me guilty-
From five to fifty years in the pen.

I took the "rap" like good people,
And never one "squawk" did I make
Jack "dropped himself" on the promise
That we make a "sensational break".

Well, to shorten a sad lengthy story,
Five years have gone over my head
Without even so much as a letter-
At first I thought he was dead.

But not long ago I discovered;
From a gal in the joint named Lyle,
That Jack and his "moll" had "got over"
And were living in true "gangster style".

If he had returned to me sometime,
Though he hadn't a cent to give
I'd forget all the hell that he's caused me,
And love him as long as I lived.

But there's no chance of his ever coming,
For he and his moll have no fears
But that I will die in this prison,
Or "flatten" this fifty years.

Tommorow I'll be on the "outside"
And I'll "drop myself" on it today,
I'll "bump 'em if they give me the "hotsquat"
On this island out here in the bay...

The iron doors swung wide next morning

For a gruesome woman of waste,
Who at last had a chance to "fix it"
Murder showed in her cynical face.

Not long ago I read in the paper
That a gal on the East Side got "hot"
And when the smoke finally retreated,
Two of gangdom were found "on the spot".

It related the colorful story
Of a "jilted gangster gal"
Two days later, a "sub-gun" ended
The story of "Suicide Sal".

Bibliography

Barrow, Blanche Caldwell and John Neal Phillips. My Life with Bonnie and Clyde. (Norman: University of Oklahoma Press, 2004.)

Burrough, Bryan. Public Enemies. (New York: The Penguin Press, 2004.)

Friedman, Lester D., Bonnie and Clyde. (BFI Publishing. 2000.)

Guinn, Jeff. Go Down Together: The True, Untold Story of Bonnie and Clyde. (New York: Simon & Schuster, 2009.)

Hinton, Ted & Grove Larry, Ambush; The Real Story of Bonnie and Clyde.

Knight, James R. and Jonathan Davis. Bonnie and Clyde: A Twenty-First-Century Update. (Austin, TX: Eakin Press, 2003.)

Milner, E.R. The Lives and Times of Bonnie and Clyde. (Carbondale and Edwardsville: Southern Illinois University Press, 1996.)

Nash, Jay Robert, Bloodletters and Badmen. (New York: M. Evans & Co., 1995.)

Parker, Emma Krause, Nell Barrow Cowan and Jan I. Fortune. The True Story of Bonnie and Clyde. (New York: New American Library, 1968.)

Penn, Arthur, Bonnie and Clyde. Edited by Lester D. Friedman. (Cambridge University Press. 2000.)

Phillips, John Neal. Running with Bonnie and Clyde, the Ten Fast Years of Ralph Fults.

(Norman: University of Oklahoma Press, 1996, 2002)

Ramsey, Winston G., ed. On The Trail of Bonnie and Clyde. (London: After The Battle Books, 2003).

Steele, Phillip, and Marie Barrow Scoma. The Family Story of Bonnie and Clyde. (Gretna, LA: Pelican Publishing Company, 2000.)

Toland, John, The Dillinger Days. (New York: Random House, 1963.)

Treherne, John. The Strange History of Bonnie and Clyde. (New York: Stein and Day, 1984.)

Made in the USA
Middletown, DE
23 June 2016